CW01478710

MONSEN AND BAER, Inc.

The Wonder of Perfume

Perfume Bottle Auction XIV

April 30, 2004.

Auctioneers: Michael DeFina, VA Lic. 2037
and Randall B. Monsen, VA Lic. 2626

Auction:
Hyatt Regency Reston Hotel
1800 Presidents Street - Reston, Virginia 22090 USA

Auction Preview: All lots will be available for viewing
and inspection from 10:00 AM to 5:00 PM on Friday, April 30, 2004.
Sale will begin at 5:00 PM, April 30, 2004.

**Monsen and Baer, Inc.
Box 529
Vienna, VA 22183 USA
(703) 938-2129 Fax (703) 242-1357
email: monsenbaer@erols.com**

ISBN #1-928655-04-1

Copyright 2004 © Monsen and Baer, all rights reserved.

None of the photographs and text in this book may be reproduced by any means including hardcopy, electronic and in cyberspace unless the expressed permission of Monsen and Baer has been obtained in writing.

The Wonder of Perfume

Table of Contents

MONSEN AND BAER PERFUME BOTTLE AUCTION FOURTEEN

Preface

To our fellow collectors in this country and abroad, greetings and good wishes! This is the fourteenth fully catalogued auction of perfume bottles produced by Monsen and Baer. This auction serves to support the International Perfume Bottle Association in that it is held during the annual IPBA Convention, and that a portion of the proceeds of the auction will be accorded to that organization. If you are a serious collector of perfume bottles, you should become a member of the IPBA, the International Perfume Bottle Association. Randall Monsen is a past president of the IPBA, and Rod Baer has served two terms as Publications Chair. The IPBA publishes a wonderful *Perfume Bottle Quarterly,* a Membership Directory, and organizes an outstanding annual Convention. We will happily send membership information and a sample of the *Perfume Bottle Quarterly* to all who request it.

The Wonder of Perfume follows upon the success of our previous books, beginning with *The Beauty of Perfume* in 1996 and following our 2003 book, *A Passion for Perfume Bottles.* As in all our previous books, we have tried to give our readers a valuable resource for perfume bottle collecting. Over the last fourteen years, Monsen and Baer publications have given collectors dozens of valuable research articles on the history of perfume companies and glass makers, in addition to photos and descriptions of thousands of perfume bottles.

The Wonder of Perfume offers collectors an astonishing array of perfume bottles and atomizers by the American companies DeVilbiss, Pyramid, and Volupté, as well as an astonishing array of rarities of the commercial type, particularly in the categories of Baccarat and Lalique. The auction will finish with a tour de force of Czechoslovakian bottles.

Our overall goal in publishing books on perfume bottles is to provide the collector with a resource for collecting and research that can be used over and over again, not only on the documentation of perfume bottles and their current value, but also on their history and their makers. The hardcover book format provides a durable object for collectors to use and re-use. Our goal here goes beyond merely selling perfume bottles, though of course we wish to do that and to do it well. In a very real sense, we want to produce for collectors something that we, as collectors ourselves, would value and find useful—something we would want to own and keep on our bookshelf. Our sincere wish is that other collectors use it, learn from it, and enjoy it. What we have said in the past bears repeating here: *Knowledge–and the sharing of it–enhances the pleasure of collecting.*

We have both been collectors since early childhood—collectors of many disparate things, not just perfume bottles. A current passion for both of us is American art pottery, in particular the Roseville Pottery and other potteries of Ohio. We have spent a lot of time thinking about the art of collecting. Why do we collect? How can we have more enjoyment collecting? What advice should we give to new collectors? Collecting is an art which has as its first rule that there are no absolute rules. Each collector must decide for herself or himself what to collect and how to go about collecting it. It follows that there are as many different collections as there are collectors. Some collectors collect only commercial perfumes, some only those that are not commercial, some collect miniature perfumes, some only the larger ones. Some collect only a very specific type and others collect anything they find that gives them pleasure. Nonetheless, it

seems wise to us to recommend something to our fellow collectors. *First, buy books. Spend some of the collecting budget on books.* An investment in knowledge is always worthwhile, and generally the book will pay for itself in short time. Books will help one to identify objects that definitely should be acquired and others that may be passed. Books will help one avoid mistakes. But probably most important is this: knowledge increases one's pleasure, and if collecting is not about pleasure it is about nothing at all. A second piece of advice for collectors is to build quality into the collection, regardless of what type of collection it is. *Quality is more important than quantity—vastly more important.* Building quality into a collection means selecting objects of known quality and paying a fair price for them. We believe that as the twenty-first century unfolds, collectors will look back longingly and wistfully upon this sale as an opportunity to acquire incredibly desirable perfume bottles at advantageous prices. Our hope is that each collector of today will also recognize this opportunity to acquire a wonderful perfume bottle for their collection.

If you have a truly special perfume bottle that you would consider selling, then our year 2005 auction, to be held in Dallas, Texas, in May, 2005, may be the perfect venue to do so. Monsen and Baer can showcase your bottle in a book which becomes a permanent part of the literature on perfume bottles, and which can then be seen by everyone for decades to come. We also purchase bottles and sometimes entire collections directly, for those who prefer an immediate sale. For those who would like to consign bottles for the year 2005 auction, please contact us *soon after this sale.* Consignment details will be sent to those who request this information. The consignment deadline is December 31, 2004, but many categories fill up *long* before that date.

The collecting of perfume bottles has enriched our lives immeasurably. First, there is the excitement of discovering and purchasing each new bottle. Then there is the joy of seeing, holding, and owning these beautiful objects, a joy that never weakens or grows old. We even enjoy selling some of them, and seeing what pleasure they will give to another collector. And in addition to all this, there are many personal relationships we have developed through this wonderful hobby, and maybe that is the greatest benefit. Thus, collecting perfume bottles has given us much, and we wish in turn to strengthen and enrich this pleasureful pastime. When we began the Monsen and Baer perfume bottle auction twelve years ago, we had little idea where it would lead us, or of the vast amount of work that would eventually be required to produce a hard-cover book such as *The Wonder of Perfume.* But this journey has been worthwhile, and we have grown to meet the challenges of each new year. We will continue to try to improve our publications as well as the quality of the bottles we offer for sale. We want everyone to know that we have written this book with great joy, and we sincerely hope that it will also bring enjoyment, knowledge, and a deepened appreciation of this wonderful collecting field to our fellow collectors. *To each of our readers: may your collections grow in quality, and may there be no limit to the pleasure you derive. Enjoy!*

Randy Monsen

Rod Baer

The Conditions of Sale
All lots sold in this auction are subject to the following conditions: please read carefully.

Terms of Sale. All lots will be sold, in the numerical sequence of this catalogue, to the highest bidder as determined by the auctioneer. In the case of disputed bids, the auctioneer shall have the sole discretion of determining the purchaser, and may elect to reoffer the lot for sale. We will accept cash, travelers checks, or personal checks with acceptable identification or if the buyer is known to us; we reserve the right in some cases to ship the lot to the purchaser after their check has cleared. Credit card sales are welcome.

Sales Tax. All lots are subject to Virginia state sales tax unless a valid tax exemption form has been filed with us; proof of sales tax exemption status may be required, i.e., a xerox copy of your sales tax registration form.

Absentee Bids. A form for absentee bids is available. We will be happy to execute your bid for you as if you were present at the auction. When you do this, it does not mean that the bidding will commence with your bid, it simply means that we will not bid for you above the amount you indicate. It is advantageous to place these absentee bids as early as possible. In the case of identical bids, the bid from the floor will take precedence; for identical absentee bids, the earlier-dated bid will take precedence. Please read shipping information below.
Telephone Bids: A very limited number of telephone lines may be available for telephone bidding. There is a $50 non-refundable fee for telephone bidding, which must be arranged two weeks prior to the auction--no exceptions.

Bidding Increments. Bidding increments are totally at the discretion of the auctioneer. However, the following increments are typically used: under $50, increments of $5; $50-$300, increments of $10; $300-$500, increments of $25; $500-$1,000, increments of $50; $1,000-$3,000, increments of $100; $3,000-$5,000, increments of $250; $5,000-$10,000, increments of $500; above $10,000, increments of $1,000.

Shipping and Handling Fees. We offer the possibility of shipping your purchases. For the United States and Canada, the flat charge for this service is **$15 per lot** for lots whose sale price is less than $1000; the charges will be higher for the lots valued over $1000 due to insurance charges. Lots which consist of large items can be shipped, with actual shipping charges to be paid by the purchaser.

Shipping purchases to Europe is also possible. **There is an initial charge of $75 for this service; additional lots will be included at the actual shipping cost, which may go above that amount if several lots are purchased.** Absentee bidders will be sent an invoice for the shipping charges and balance due; we offer the convenience of accepting payment in all major European currencies. We normally use United Parcel Service or DHL to ship to Europe, and in most cases we cannot use the Postal Service. United Parcel Service is highly reliable and extremely rapid. However, please note that the minimum charge for a small parcel sent by UPS to Europe is $75. Parcels consisting of several lots may cost twice that amount. Lots which are shipped outside the United States are subject to customs duties in the destination country, which is based upon the purchase price of the lot and we are required to state it. It is the responsibility of the purchaser to determine the amount of these duties and to pay them in full.

Price Estimates and Reserves. Some lots are offered for sale with a "reserve price." The reserve is a confidential minimum price below which the lot will not be sold. The reserve price for any lot in this sale is usually well below the low estimate and is never allowed to be higher than the estimates. The estimates are merely a range within which we believe the lot may find a buyer, but of course many lots may be sold at prices well below or well above these estimates, depending on the wishes of the bidders.

Buyer's Premium. A buyer's premium of **15%** will be added to the hammer price of all lots, to be paid by the buyer as a part of the purchase price.

Condition of Lots. While we attempt to describe the condition of each lot as accurately as possible, as in all auctions, the lots here are sold "as is." We attempt to mention in the descriptions any negative aspect we think bidders need to know, for example: [label absent], [chip to stopper], etc. However, many factors relating to condition cannot be adequately described in the short captions of this catalogue, and this is especially true in the case of miniature or group lots. Very many perfume bottles have exceedingly tiny chips around the opening where the stopper enters the bottle. Sometimes these may also be found on the tongue of the stopper or on the base of the bottle. The boxes and labels of commercial bottles all show varying signs of usage and age, such as discoloration and fraying, and unless we note that the box is in pristine condition, such signs of age should be expected. All bottles, and especially commercial ones, may contain perfume residue and other internal stains. Not all stoppers fit into the bottle with perfect snugness and symmetry, especially those of Czechoslovakian manufacture. Therefore, bidders should inspect each lot they wish to bid on prior to purchase. We would also be happy to discuss the condition of any lot prior to the sale. Unless stated otherwise, the bottles are empty of perfume.
    Note on the sizes of bottles: The photographs in this catalogue depict the lots as clearly as possible. However, most photographs show the bottles *smaller* than they actually are, and some photos, especially the full page portraits, may show the bottles *larger* than they actually are. Read the lot descriptions to know the actual sizes. Measurements given in this catalogue are in inches and centimeters, rounded in most cases to the nearest quarter inch or half-centimeter.
    In cases where glass by a particular maker is described as unsigned, the catalogue can only provide a reasonable surmise, not a guarantee, as to the maker. Many of the early French glass makers produced glass of similar quality and design. In these cases, the buyer should consult the available reference works and thereafter make their own determination. The glass made by Lalique & Cie. is all grouped together; this includes bottles designed after René Lalique's death by Marc and Marie Claude Lalique. Following the convention used in Utt [1990], perfume bottles produced for sale by R. Lalique & Cie. are referred to as Maison Lalique or Cristal Lalique.
    Reference numbers are provided for Lalique, Baccarat, and in many cases for Czech glass and commercial bottles, as described in Utt [1990], Compagnie des Cristalleries de Baccarat [1986], North [1990], Forsythe I & II [1982 & 1993], Lefkowith [1994], and Leach [1997]. These reference numbers are used throughout the catalogue.

Consignments. We will be accepting consignments for our fifteenth auction, to be held May 2005, and we are particularly in search of fine perfume bottles. Our rates of consignment are very competitive with other auctions, and we can offer exposure of your bottles to a specialized buying audience. We guarantee confidentiality. We also purchase individual bottles or entire collections outright, if that avenue of sale is preferred. Contact us and we would be happy to discuss these terms with you. We are especially interested in perfume bottles of high quality, not broken or damaged pieces. Please bear in mind that consignments for the year 2005 auction must be completed by December 31, 2004 to allow sufficient time to prepare and publish the catalogue; many categories fill up well before that date.

Bibliography on the Collection of Perfume

L'Argus des Ventes aux Enchères Valentine's: Verrerie. Paris: Dorotheum Editions, 2000.

Atlas, M. and Monniot, A. Guerlain - Les Flacons à Parfum Depuis 1828. Toulouse, France: Editions Milan, 1997.

Atlas, M. and Monniot, A. Un Siècle d'Echantillons Guerlain. Toulouse, France: Editions Milan, 1995.

Ball, J. D. and Torem, D. H. Commercial Fragrance Bottles. Atglen, Pennsylvania: Schiffer Publishing Co., 1993.

Ball, J. D. and Torem, D. H. Fragrance Bottle Masterpieces. Atglen, Pennsylvania: Schiffer Publishing Co., 1996.

Barlow, Raymond E., and Kaiser, Joan E. A Guide to Sandwich Glass: Vases, Colognes, and Stoppers. West Chester, Pa: Schiffer Publishing, 1987.

Barille, Elisabeth. Coty. Paris: Editions Assouline, 1995.

Berger, C. & D. Tous les Parfums du Monde. Toulouse: Editions Milan, 1995.

Bonduelle, J. P. et Lancry, J. M. Flacons à Parfums Catalogues pour les Ventes aux Enchères Publiques: March 31, 1990; March 24, 1991; June 16, 1991; October 24, 1991; June 21, 1992; May 16, 1993; November 21, 1993; March 27, 1994; November 20, 1994; June 18, 1995; December 3, 1995; June 16, 1996; December 1, 1996; June 15, 1997; December 7, 1997; November 25, 2000; expert: J.-M. Martin-Hattemberg.

Bonhams Scent Bottle and Lalique auction catalogues. November 29, 1989; October 18, 1990; November 21, 1990; April 24, 1991; October 24, 1991; October 28, 1991; April 28, 1992; October 29, 1992; April 7, 1993; June 28, 1993; October 20, 1993; expert: Juliette Bogaers; September 29, 1997; experts Isobel Muston, Eric Knowles, and Emma Thommeret.

Bowman, Glinda. Miniature Perfume Bottles. Atglen, Pennsylvania: Schiffer, 1994.

Brine, Lynda and Whitaker, Nancy. Scent Bottles Through the Ages: An A - Z Pictorial. Bath, UK: Brine and Whitaker, 1998.

Byrd, Joan. DeVilbiss Perfumizers & Perfume Lights: The Harvey K. Littleton Collection. Cullowhee, North Carolina: Western Carolina University, 1985.

Cabré, M., Sebbag, M., Vidal, V.. Femmes de Papier - Perfumed Cards. Toulouse: Editions Milan, 1998.

Cabré, Monique. La Légende du Chevalier d'Orsay: Parfums de Dandy. Toulouse: Editions Milan, 1997.

Camard. Prestige de la Parfumerie. Paris, June 5, 2003. Expert: J.-M. Marti-Hattemberg.

Charles-Roux, Edmonde. Chanel and Her World. New York: Vendome Press, 1981.

Chassaing, Rivet, Fournié. Flacons à Parfums Catalogue pour la Vente aux Enchères Publiques. June 27, 1994, Toulouse, France; expert: Geneviève Fontan.

Christie's South Kensington. Lalique including the Pickard-Cambridge Collection of Lalique Scent Bottles, May 12, 2000.

Christin, Jean. Flacons à parfum du XXe siècle. September 29, 1996, Hotel des Bergues, Geneva, Switzerland.

Clements, M. L. and Clements, P. R. Avon Collectible Fashion Jewelry and Awards. Atglen, PA: Schiffer & Co., 1998.

Cohet et Feraud Floréal Perfume Bottle Auction Catalogue. Toulouse, France, April 15-16, 1995; November 4, 1995; expert: Flora Entajan.

Colard, Grégoire. [Caron] The Secret Charm of a Perfumed House. Paris: J. C. Lattès, 1984.

Compagnie des Cristalleries de Baccarat. Baccarat Les Flacons à Parfum/The Perfume Bottles. Paris: Henri Addor & Associés, 1986.

Courset, J-M. 5000 Miniatures de Parfum. Toulouse: Editions Milan, 1995.

Courset, J-M, and Dekindt, P.. 6000 Miniatures de Parfum. Toulouse: Editions Milan, 1998.

Coutau-Bégarie, O. Flacons à Parfums Catalogues pour les Ventes aux Enchères Publiques: December 6, 1993; October 24, 1994; June 12, 1995; November 27, 1995; June 3, 1996; December 1, 1997; November 16, 1998; June 7, 1999; April 17, 2000; November 6, 2000; November 18, 2002; expert: Régine de Robien.

Demornex, Jacqueline. Lancôme. Paris: Editions du Regard, 1985.

Doyle New York. Belle Epoque sales of February 7, 2001; June 6, 2001. Expert: Eric Silver

Drouot-Richelieu, Neret-Minet, Coutau-Begarie. Flacons à Parfums Catalogues pour les Ventes aux Enchères Publiques: June 23, 1986; April 2, 1987; Nov. 4, 1987; April 13, 1988; Nov. 7, 1988; May 20, 1989; Nov. 13, 1989; May 21, 1990; Nov. 24, 1990; April 8, 1991; May 27, 1991; Nov. 15, 1991; December 14, 1992; expert: Régine de Robien.

Drouot-Richelieu, Neret-Minet. Flacons à Parfums Catalogue pour la Vente aux Enchères Publiques. December 14, 1992; expert: J.-M. Martin-Hattemberg.

Drouot-Richelieu, Millon & Robert. Flacons à Parfums: Catalogue pour la Vente aux Enchères Publiques. December 6, 1993; expert: J.-M. Martin-Hattemberg.

Duchesne, Clarence, ed. La Mémoire des Parfums, Numeros 1-11. Paris, 1988-1991.

Duval, René. Parfums de Volnay. Catalogue of the Company, 1928.

Edwards, Michael. Fragrances of the World 2000; Fragrances of the World 2001. Sydney, Australia: Michael Edwards, 2000 and 2001.

Edwards, Michael. The Fragrance Adviser 1999. Sydney, Australia: Michael Edwards, 1999.

Edwards, Michael. Perfume Legends: French Feminine Fragrances. Sydney, Australia: HM Editions, 1996.

Enghien. Flacons de Parfum. June 22, 2002. Expert: Jean-Marie Martin-Hattemberg.

Feder, Soraya. Divine Beauty: The Art of Collectibles. Paris: L'Aventurine. 2001.

Fellous, Colette. Guerlain. Paris: Denoël, 1987.

Fleck, F. Flacons à Parfum, Catalogue for the Perfume Bottle Auction, March 12, 1994; expert: Anne Meter-Seguin.

Fontan, Geneviève. Cote des Flacons de Parfum Modernes. Toulouse: Arfon, 1999.

Fontan, Geneviève. Cote Générale des Cartes Parfumées; Volume III. Toulouse: Arfon, 1997, 2000.

Fontan, Geneviève. Cote Générale des Echantillons de Parfum: Nouveautés 98; Nouveautés 99; Nouveautés 2000. Toulouse: Arfon, 1998, 1999, 2000.

Fontan, Geneviève. Echantillons Tubes de Parfum. Toulouse: Arfon, 2000.

Fontan, Geneviève. Parfums d'Extase. Toulouse: Arfon, 1996.

Fontan, Geneviève, and Barnouin, Nathalie. Cote Générale des Echantillons de Parfum. Toulouse: Editions Fontan & Barnouin, 1996.

Fontan, Geneviève, and Barnouin, Nathalie. L'Argus des Echantillons de Parfum. Toulouse: Editions Milan, 1992.

Fontan, Geneviève, and Barnouin, Nathalie. La Cote Internationale des Echantillons de Parfum, 1995-1996. Les Echantillons Anciens. Toulouse: 813 Edition, 1994.

Fontan, Geneviève, and Barnouin, Nathalie. La Cote Internationale des Echantillons de Parfums Modernes. Toulouse: 813 Edition, 1995.

Fontan, Geneviève, and Barnouin, Nathalie. Les Intégrales: Rochas and Les Intégrales: Ricci. Toulouse: Editions Fontan & Barnouin, 1996.

Forsythe, Ruth. Made in Czechoslovakia. Marietta, Ohio: Richardson Printing Co., 1982; Made in Czechoslovakia, Book 2. Marietta Ohio: Richardson Printing Co., 1993.

Frankl, Beatrice. Parfum-Flacons. Augsburg: Battenberg Verlag, 1994.

Gardiner Houlgate. Perfume Bottles, Sale 6001 [UKPBCC]. October 3, 1998. Expert: Lynda Brine.

Gerson, Roselyn. Vintage Ladies' Compacts. Paducah, KY: Collector Books, 1996.

Gerson, Roselyn. Vintage and Contemporary Purse Accessories. Paducah, KY: Collector Books, 1997.

Ghozland, F. Perfume Fantasies. Toulouse: Editions Milan, 1987.

Green, Annette, and Dyett, Linda. Secrets of Aromatic Jewelry. Paris, New York: Flammarion, 1998.

Guinn, Hugh D. The Glass of René Lalique at Auction. Tulsa, Oklahoma: Guindex Publications, 1992.

Hymne au Parfum: Catalogue of the exposition, 1990-1991. Paris: Comité Français du Parfum, 1991.

Johnson, Frances. Compacts, Powder, and Paint. Atglen, PA: Schiffer Publishing, 1996.

Jones-North, Jacquelyne. Czechoslovakian Perfume Bottles and Boudoir Accessories. Marietta, Ohio: Antique Publications, 1990; revised editon, 1999.

Kaufman, William I. Perfume. New York: E. P. Dutton & Co., 1974.

Killian, E. H. Perfume Bottles Remembered. Traverse City, Michigan: E. Killian, 1989.

La Quinzaine du Parfum. Perfume Bottle Auction Catalogue for the sale of October 21, 1994; expert: Creezy Courtoy. Brussels, Belgium.

Latimer, Tirza True. The Perfume Atomizer: An Object with Atmosphere. West Chester, Pennsylvania: Schiffer Publishing, 1991.

Leach, Ken. Perfume Presentation: 100 Years of Artistry. Toronto: Kres Publishing, 1997.

Lefkowith, Christie Mayer. The Art of Perfume. New York: Thames and Hudson, 1994.

Lefkowith, Christie Mayer. Masterpieces of the Perfume Industry. New York: Editions Stylissimo, 2000.

Lefkowith, Christie Mayer. Perfume Presentations Auction. 8 November, 2003, Geneva Switzerland..

Le Louvre des Antiquaires. Autour du Parfum du XVIe au XIXe Siècle. Paris: Le Louvre des Antiquaires, 1985.

Marcilhac, Félix. R. Lalique: Catalogue Raisonné de l'Oeuvre de Verre. Paris: Editions de l'Amateur, 1989.

Marsh, Madeleine. Perfume Bottles: A Collector's Guide. London: Octopus, Ltd, 1999.

Martin, Hazel. Figural Perfume and Scent Bottles. Lancaster, CA: Hazel Martin, 1982.

Martin-Hattemberg, Jean-Marie. Caron. Toulouse: Milan Editions, 2000.

Martin-Hattemberg, Jean-Marie. Le parfum histoire et expertise, Revue Experts, #42, March 1999.

Martin-Hattemberg, Jean-Marie. Précieux Effluves / Scentsfully Precious. Toulouse: Milan Editions, 1997.

Matthews, Leslie G. The Antiques of Perfume. London: G. Bell & Sons, 1973.

Mini Flacons. Wiesbaden, Germany: SU Verlag, 1993.

Morris, Edwin T. Scents of Time: Perfume from Ancient Egypt to the 21st Century. New York: Metropolitan Museum of Art, 1999.

Mouillefarine, Laurence. Objets de la Beauté à Collectionner. Boulogne, France: Éditions MDM, 1999.

Mueller, Laura M. Collector's Encyclopedia of Compacts: Volumes 1 and 2. Paducah, KY: Collector Books, 1996.

Neret-Minet. Flacons à Parfums Catalogue pour les Ventes aux Enchères Publiques, November 14, 1991; expert: Elisabeth Danenberg.

North, Jacquelyne. Commercial Perfume Bottles. West Chester, Pennsylvania: Schiffer Publishing Co, 1987.

North, Jacquelyne. Perfume, Cologne, and Scent Bottles. West Chester, Pennsylvania: Schiffer Publishing Co, 1986.

La Parfumerie Française et L'Art dans la Présentation. La Revue des Marques de la Parfumerie et de la Savonnerie. Paris, 1925.

Parfum, Art, et Valeur. Catalogue de Vente, November 15, 1995. Expert: Geneviève Fontan.

Paulson, Paul L. Guide to Russian Silver Hallmarks. Paulson: Washington DC, 1976.

Pavia, Fabienne. The World of Perfume. New York: Knickerbocker Press, 1995.

Perfume Bottle Quarterly, Volumes 1-15. International Perfume Bottle Association.

Phillips Auctions. Perfume Presentations. October 6, 1996, October 26, 1997; October 25, 1998. Geneva, Switzerland. Expert: Christie Mayer Lefkowith. Perfume Presentations. November 27, 1999. Zürich, Switzerland; December 10, 2000, New York. Expert: Ken Leach.

René Lalique and Cristal Lalique Perfume Bottles (The Weinstein Collection). New York: Christie's/Lalique Society of America, 1993.

René Lalique et Cie. Lalique Glass: The Complete Illustrated Catalogue for 1932. Reprinted by The Corning Museum of Glass, Corning, New York. New York. Dover Publications, 1981.

Restrepo, Federico. Le Livre d'Heures des Flacons et des Rêves. Toulouse: Editions Milan, 1995.

Scent Bottles Through the Centuries: the Collection of Joan Hermanowski. St. Petersburg, Florida: Museum of Fine Art, 1997.

Sloan, Jean. Perfume and Scent Bottle Collecting. Lombard, Illinois: Wallace-Homestead Co., 1986.

Sotheby's New York. Important Twentieth Century Decorative Works of Art, including the Mary Lou and Glenn Utt Collection of Lalique. New York, December 4-5, 1998.

Taylor, Pamela F. Heavenly Scents. Privately published, UK, 2000.

Truitt, R. and D. Czech Glass 1918-1939. Glass Collector's Digest, Vol. 10, #6, May 1997. pp. 39-46.

Utt, Mary Lou and Glenn. Lalique Perfume Bottles. New York: Crown Publishers, 1990. Updated Addendum Listing and Photo Supplement, 2001.

Watine-Arnault, Jean. Flacons à Parfums Christian Dior: Catalogue pour la Vente aux Enchères Publiques. April 12, 1992; expert: Régine de Robien.

Whitmyer, M. & K. Bedroom and Bathroom Glassware of the Depression Years. Paducah, Kentucky: Collector Books, 1990.

Important Books Available from Monsen and Baer:

The Legend of the Chevalier d'Orsay: Parfums de Dandy [M. Cabré] @ $48 + $7 shipping. Text in French and in English, Hardcover§

Made in Czechoslovakia, Book 2 [R. Forsythe] @ $29.95 + $5 shipping. Softcover¶

Perfume, Cologne, and Scent Bottles [J. Jones-North] @ $69.95 + $7 shipping. Hardcover§

We can ship the above books to Europe, but the airmail cost is as follows: §These books can be shipped for an additional $35 each; ¶These books can be shipped for an additional $18 each.

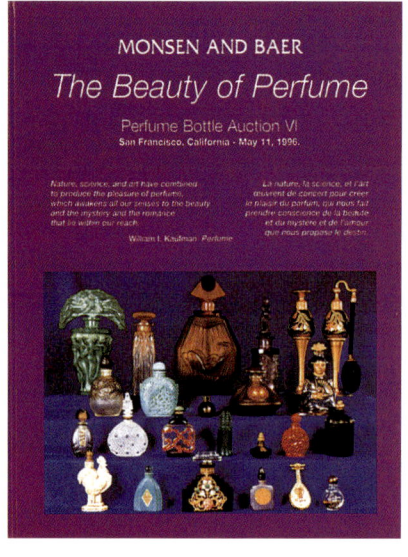

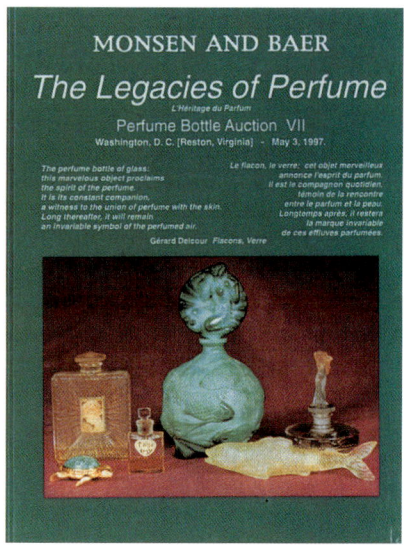

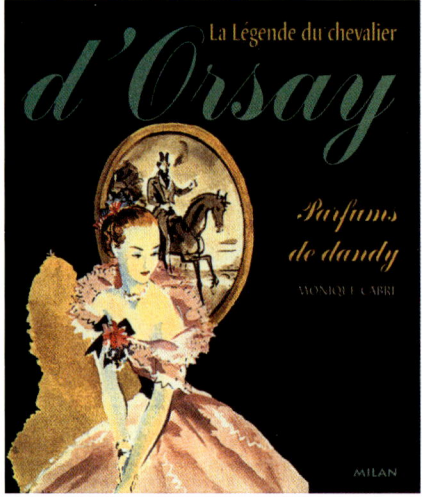

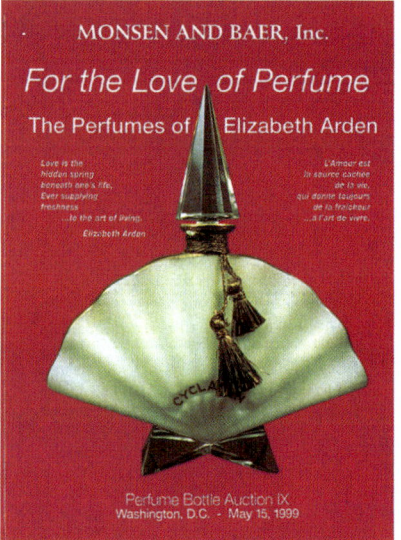

The Legend of the Chevalier d'Orsay: Parfums de Dandy, by Monique Cabré. A history of d'Orsay, beautifully illustrated, with text in English and French, Hardcover, 126 pp. Price: $48, plus $7 shipping.

Monsen and Baer publish these books on American Art Pottery: *The Collectors' Compendium of Roseville Pottery, Volumes I and II.*

These books include new historical research and color photos of all the pieces in the pottery lines covered. Price guide information is included in Volume I and a separate price guide accompanies Volume II. Both books are 128 pp each, hardcover, and prices are postpaid. Volume III will be available summer 2000.

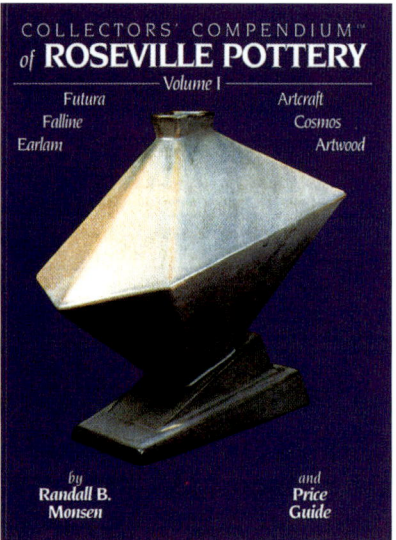

Volume I - $35

Volume II - $45

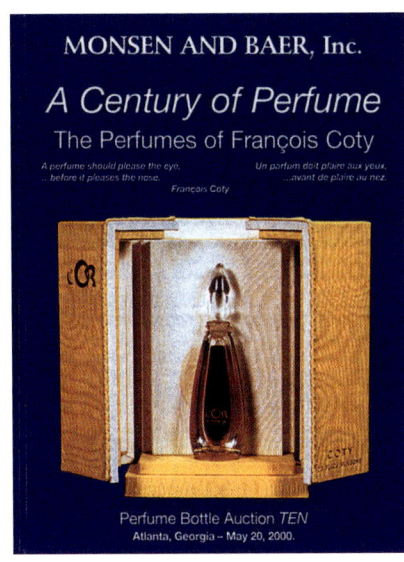

These Monsen and Baer Publications are available, all with prices realized:

[Shipping: $4.50 for first one, $3.00 for each additional title]:

SOFT COVER

Monsen and Baer Perfume Bottle Auction I, Chicago, April 6, 1991 @ $18.00. ($25 for International shipment).

Monsen and Baer Perfume Bottle Auction II, Atlanta, May 16, 1992 @ $25.00. ($30 for International shipment).

Monsen and Baer Perfume Bottle Auction III, Dallas, May 1, 1993 @ $28.00. ($35 for International shipment).

Monsen and Baer Perfume Bottle Auction IV, Washington, D. C., May 14, 1994 @ $29.00. ($35 for International shipment).

Monsen and Baer Perfume Bottle Auction V, Chicago, Illinois, May 6, 1995 @ $35.00. ($40 for International shipment).

HARD COVER

The Beauty of Perfume, Monsen and Baer Perfume Bottle Auction VI, San Francisco, California, May 11, 1996. @ $35.00. ($45 for International)

The Legacies of Perfume, Monsen and Baer Perfume Bottle Auction VII, Washington D. C., May 3, 1997. @ $45.00 ($50 for International shipment.)

Memories of Perfume, Monsen and Baer Perfume Bottle Auction VIII, Chicago, Illinois., May 16, 1998. @ $45.00 ($50 for International shipment.)

For the Love of Perfume, Monsen and Baer Perfume Bottle Auction IX, Washington, D. C., May 15, 1999. @ $45.00 ($60 for International shipment.)

A Century of Perfume, Monsen and Baer Perfume Bottle Auction X, Atlanta, Georgia, May 20, 2000. @ $45.00 ($60 for International shipment.)

The Magic of Perfume, Monsen and Baer Perfume Bottle Auction XI, Santa Clara, California, May 18, 2001. @ $45.00 ($65 for International shipment.)

The Joy of Collecting Perfume Bottles, Monsen and Baer Perfume Bottle Auction XII, Dallas, Texas, May 17, 2002. @ $45.00 ($65 for International shipment.)

A Passion for Perfume Bottles, Monsen and Baer Perfume Bottle Auction XIII, Orlando, Florida, May 16, 2003. @ $45.00 ($65 for International shipment.)

The Wonder of Perfume, Monsen and Baer Perfume Bottle Auction XIV, Washington D.C., April 30, 2004. @ $45.00 ($65 for International shipment.)

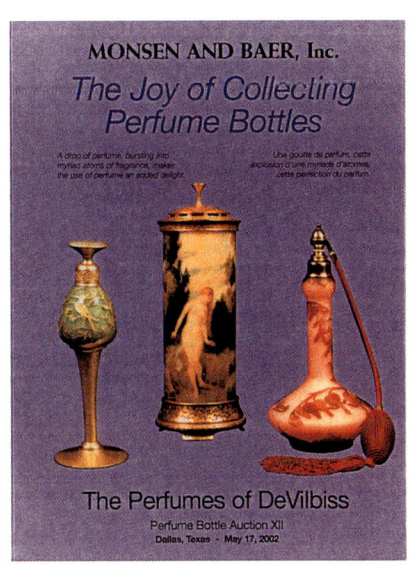

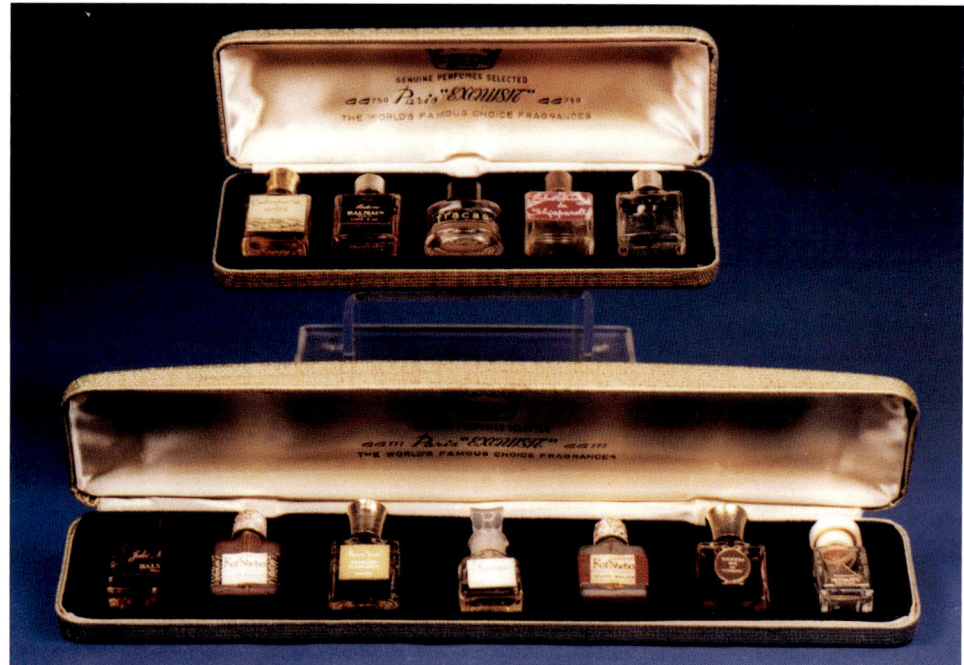

Lot #1. Paris *Exquisit* set of seven: Balmain *Jolie Madame;* Capucci *Parce Que!;* Corday *Toujours Moi;* Judith Muller *Bat Sheba Exotic Oriental* and *Woody Modern;* Raphael *Réplique;* Revlon *Intimate;* Paris *Exquisit* set of five: Balmain *Jolie Madame;* Gres *Cabochard;* Piguet *Fracas;* Pucci *Vivara;* Schiaparelli *Shocking.* Two sets. Est. $100.00-$200.00.

Lot #2. Fragonard *Billet Doux, Caresse, Reve Indien, Murmure, Baroque*—two of each—in their box; Fragonard *Emilie, Fragonard, Melodie; Murmure, Reve de Grasse,* in their box. 2 items. Est. $100.00-$200.00.

Lot #3. Bourjois *On the Wind*, Corday *Possession*, Guerlian *Nahema*, Lenthéric *Tweed*, Matchabelli *Cachet, Golden Autumn, Stradivari,* and *Windsong*, Raphael *Plaisir* [2], Ricci *Capricci*, Shulton *Early American Old Spice*, Vigny *Heure Intime*, Von Furstenberg *Tatiana*, bottle marked simply *Perfume*. Fifteen items. Est. $100.00-$200.00.

Lot #4. Paquin *9 x 9* black glass bottle and gold screw-on stopper with a blue stone, gold label on front, bottom impressed *Paquin Made in France*. Est. $100.00-$150.00.

Lot #5. Corday *Jet,* mini with black glass stopper; Matchabelli *Crown Jewel* in a cardboard case to advertise the 1952 Chevrolet and *Golden Autumn* to advertise the 1966 Chevrolet; Helena Rubenstein *Golden Autumn,* unopened, in its box; Williams *Golden Lilac;* Yardley *Bond Street;* 4711 *Mignon Lavender Salts,* in its pouch. Seven items. Est. $100.00-$200.00.

Lot #6. Avon *Charisma,* Bokay *Apple Blossom,* Cara Nome *Tish Tish,* Coty *L'Origan,* Duchess of Paris *Infatuation,* Fabergé, Kerkoff *Djer Kiss,* Lucien Lelong *Opening Night* and *Passionnement,* one unmarked, Matchabelli *Cachet* and *Golden Autumn,* Mumtaz *Sweet Pea,* Novell *Lady,* Hudnut *DuBarry* face powder, Radio Girl face powder [unopened], metal atomizer for perfume. 17 items. Est. $100.00-$200.00.

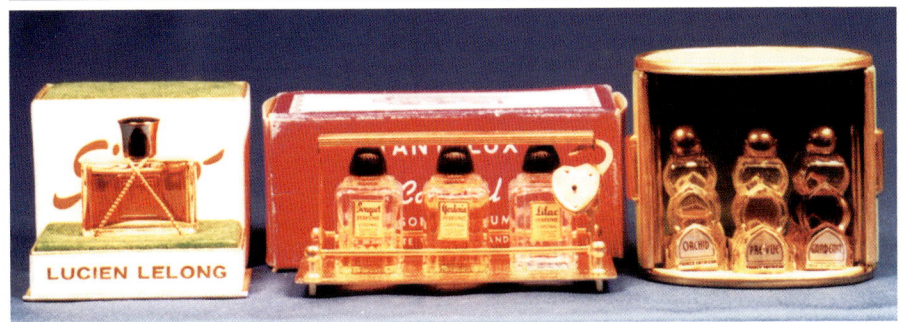

Lot #7. Cardinal *Bouquet, Gardenia, Lilac,* in their box, Franco American *Orchid, Pre-Vue, Gardenia,* in their box, Guerlian *Shalimar,* in its box, Lanvin, *Arpege, My Sin, Rumeur, Scandal,* in their box, Lucien Lelong *Sirôcco,* in its box, Lenthéric *Tweed,* in its box, Parfumerie du Val Creux *Lavande,* Roger & Gallet *Le Jade.* Eight items. Est. $200.00-$300.00.

Lot #8. Villon *Tryst* red glass bottle and black glass stopper, 2.6" [6.6 cm], the entire design resembling that of a skyscraper, empty, original label on front. Est. $150.00-$250.00.

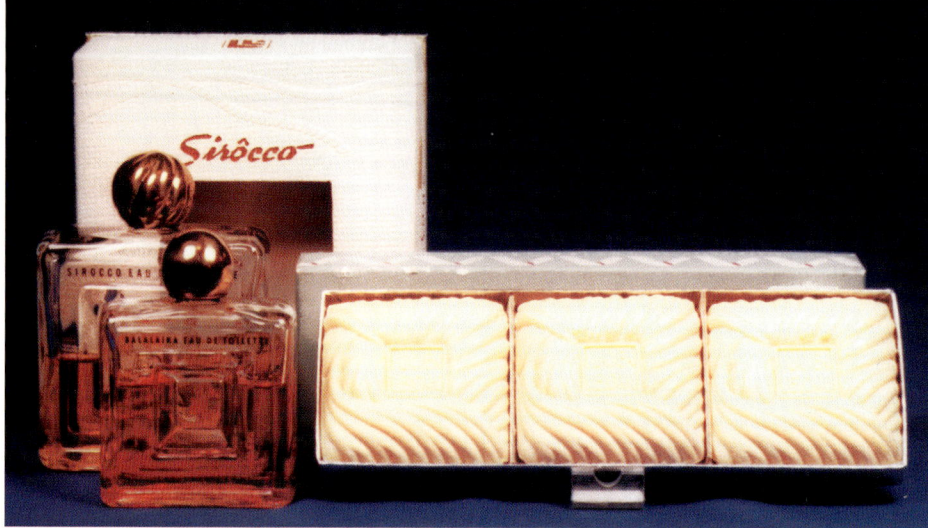

Lot #11. Karoff *Aromalite* three miniature bottles with red, black, and white caps, each 1.4" [3.5 cm], each marked *Morning, Noon, and Night*, with their label, in a lamp. Est. $50.00-$100.00.

Lot #9. Lucien Lelong *Mon Image,* 1.7" [4.3 cm], mini with gold cap, labels front and bottom, in its mirrored box; *Jabot* dress clip, 2.2" [5.6 cm] long, label on back; *Gardenia,* 2" [5.1 cm]; *Indiscret* [3 diff.]; *Orgueil* [2 diff.] *Sirocco,* 2" [5.1 cm], empty; *Tailspin; Indiscret* and *Tailspin,* 2.3" [5.8 cm] in a sachet pillow; *Balalaika* and *Sirocco,* eaux de toilette; *Honeysuckle,* set of three soaps; 4 unidentified Lelong bottles. 18 items. Est. $150.00-$300.00.

Lot #10. Carven *Robe d'un Soir;* Coty *Emeraude;* Dana *Platine;* De Rauch *Belle de Rauch;* Dior *Diorissimo* and *Miss Dior* [2 diff.]; D'Orsay *Intoxication* [4 diff.]; Evyan *Most Precious;* Fragonard *Cognac;* Houbigant *Chantilly;* Lancôme *Magie;* Lentheric *Tweed* [2 diff.]; Matchabelli *Crown Jewel* and *Golden Autumn;* Jean Patou *Joy* and *Câline;* Howard Tawes *Sweet Tobacco Blossom;* Weil *Zibeline.* 23 items. Est. $200.00-$300.00.

Lot #12. Elizabeth Arden *Mémoire Chérie* set of flower mist, hand lotion, dusting powder, soap and two bath cubes, in their plastic case with label and in their original box. Est. $125.00-$175.00.

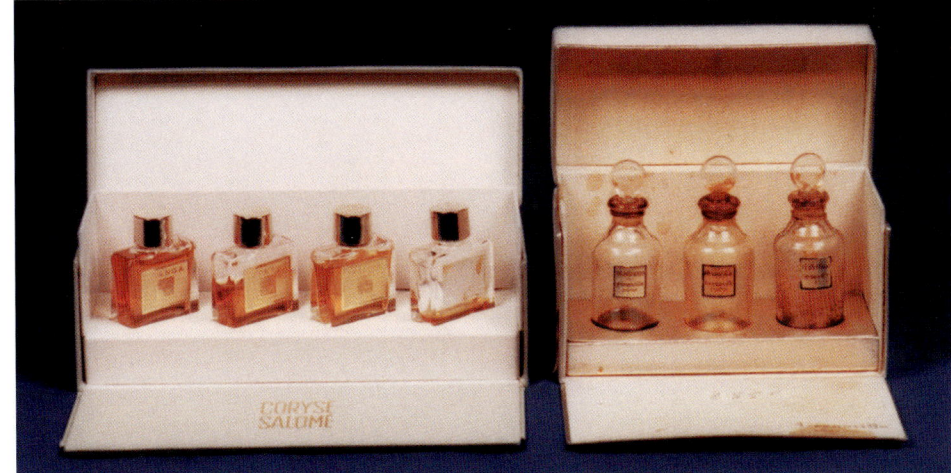

Lot 13. Coryse Salome *Epilogue, Opera, Peché Permis, Ylanga*, in their box; Grenoville *Avant L'Ete, Casanova, Oeillet Fané*, all with glass stoppers, in their box. Two items. Est. $125.00-$250.00.

Lot #14. Bourjois *Chypre* and *Evening in Paris*, perfume and cologne; Millot *Crepe de Chine;* Renaud *Sweet Pea* parfum en poudre; Shulton *Friendship's Garden;* Lucretia Vanderbilt, 2 boxes. 8 items. Est. $200.00-$350.00.

Lot #15. Balmain *Miss Balmain;* Coty *Paris* in swan and *L'Origan* in shoe; Eisenberg *Eniticing* and *Stirring;* Fath *Canasta*, in its box; Dorothy Gray *Nosegay*, in box; Karoff *On Guard* sword; 4711 *Tosca*, in its box. Eight items. Est. $150.00-$300.00.

Lot #16. Dana *Ambush* replica glass mini with gold cap, 1.6" [4.1 cm], in its box; *Platine* replica glass mini with gold cap, silver label, in its box; *Bon Voyage* clear glass mini with gold cap, red label, in its special pouch; *20 Carats* clear glass bottle with black cap, 3.1" [7.9 cm], empty; *Tabu* [two diff.] clear glass bottles with black caps. Six items. Est. $150.00-$200.00.

Lot #17. Lanvin *My Sin* small glass miniature with black cap, 1.7" [4.3 cm], in its adorable French poodle cardboard holder. Est. $150.00-$250.00.

11

Lot #19. Avon snail bottle, 2.6" [6.6 cm], full of perfume which is possibly *Charisma*. Est. $25.00-$40.00.

Lot #18. Caron *Alpona*, Cheramy *April Showers;* Duvinne *Fresh Flowers;* Forvil *5 Fleurs,* glass stopper; Fragonard *Moment Volé;* Dorothy Gray *Night Drums* and *Nosegay,* in red carrier; Houbigant *Quelques Fleurs;* Lander *Gardenia;* Lelong *Indiscret;* Lentheric *Dark Brilliance* and *Tweed* [2 diff.]; Lily Bermuda, marked IRice; Lohse *Lavender;* Lounds Pateman *Devon Violets;* Helena Rubenstein *Heaven Sent;* Vigny *Echo Troublant,* frosted glass stopper; Weil *Secret of Venus;* man in black tophat, marked *Germany;* unidentified lamp. 20 items. Est. $150.00-$300.00.

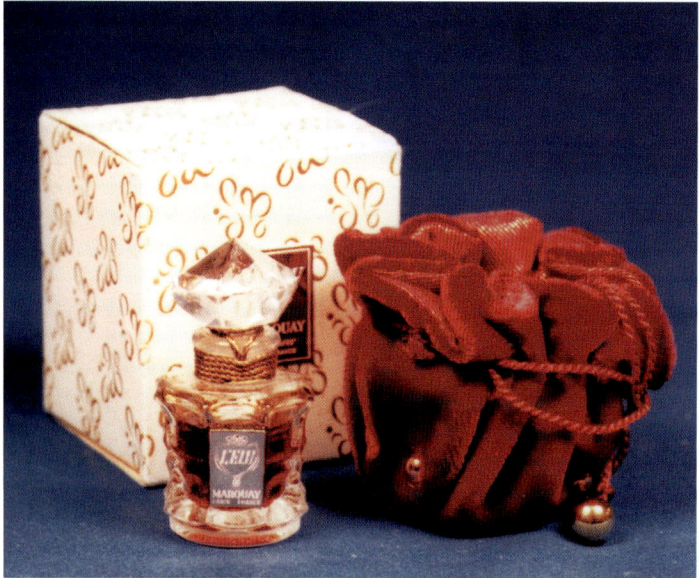

Lot #20. Marquay *L'Elu* tiny clear glass bottle and stopper, 2" [5.1 cm], of faceted shape with gold label, in its bright red pouch and box. Est. $100.00-$200.00.

Lot #21. Lentheric *Shanghai* clear glass miniature bottle and gold stopper, 1.3" [3.3 cm], in its box with cellophane front. Est. $75.00-$125.00.

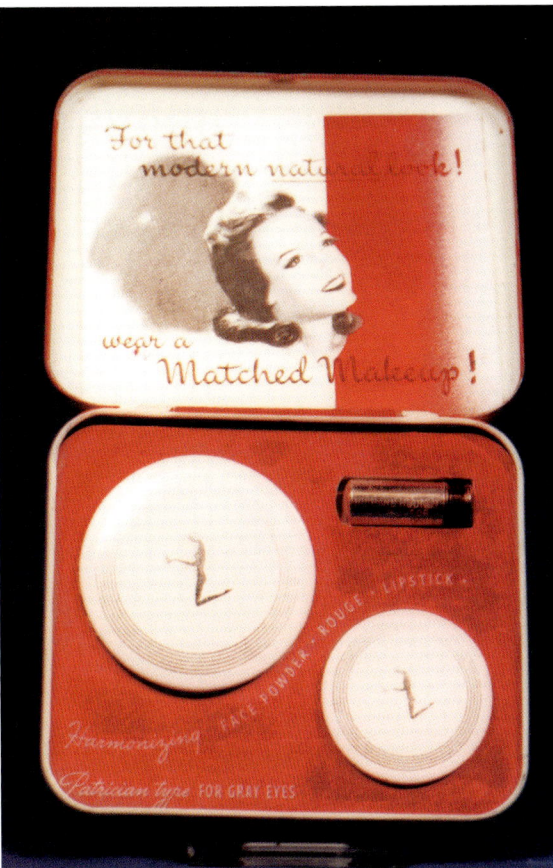

Lot #22. Richard Hudnut *Marvelous Matched Makeup* tin containing face powder, rouge, and lipstick. Est. $75.00-$150.00.

Lot #23. Ballarde *Automne en Arcadi;* Bo-Kay *Elegant* and *Sweet Pea;* Ciro with red flower stopper; Corday *Toujours Moi;* Christian Dior *Diorissimo;* Fabergé *Fabergette;* Fragonard *Belle de Nuit;* Houbigant *Presence;* Joy Time bells; Lanvin *My Sin* [2 diff.] and *Prétexte;* J. Patou *Joy;* Roger & Gallet *Fleurs d'Amour;* N. Rosenstein *Tianne* and *Odalisque;* Schiaparelli *Shocking.* 18 items. Est. $200.00-$300.00.

Lot #24. Ciro *New Horizons, Danger, Reflexions, Surrender,* four miniature glass bottles with gold metal caps, heights from 1.4" to 1.7" [3.6 to 4.3 cm], each a replica of its standard counterpart, full, in their original boxes of green, red, blue and brown. Four items. Est. $100.00-$175.00.

Lot #25. Stork Club glass bottle encased in metal with metal cap, 1.8" [4.6 cm], name and stork logo in black enamel. This miniature is quite seldom seen today. Est. $75.00-$125.00.

Lot #26. Rose Valois *Aigrette, Canotier, Marotte* [names for hats, such as 'plumed hat,' 'boater'] unusual set of six clear glass bottles with head-shaped plastic caps and six different hats, 2.4" [6 cm], in a white plastic stand and clear lucite cover, each with a label and the set with a label underneath. Rose Valois was originally known for haute couture hats; this set is quite rare. Est. $600.00-$750.00.

Lot #27. Caron *Fleurs de Rocaille* ['Rock Garden'], 2.2" [5.5 cm]; Christian Dior *Miss Dior* glass bottle and metal cap, 3.5" [8.9 cm]; Parfums Lagerfeld glass bottle and metal stopper, 1.6" [4 cm]; Guy LaRoche *Fidji,* 2.1" [5.3 cm]; Jean Patou *Câline,* 3" [7.6 cm] with metal stopper. Five items, all in their original boxes. Est. $100.00-$150.00.

Lot #28. Matchabelli *Lily of the Valley* early miniature bottle with metal crown stopper, labels front and back, unsigned. Est. $50.00-$100.00.

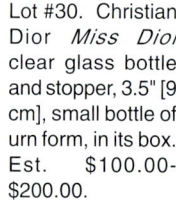

Lot #29. Matchabelli *Added Attraction* glass bottle with gold screw-on cap, 1.6" [4 cm], the bottle enameled in red and gold, gold oval label on bottom, in its original presentation box of red velvet lined with white satin. Est. $200.00-$350.00.

Lot #30. Christian Dior *Miss Dior* clear glass bottle and stopper, 3.5" [9 cm], small bottle of urn form, in its box. Est. $100.00-$200.00.

Lot #31. Mary Chess set of six clear glass bottles with gold stoppers, from 2.1" to 3.1" [5.3 to 7.8 cm], including *Carnation, Tapestry, Gardenia, Yram, Strategy,* and *White Lilac,* each with label underneath, full, in their box. Est. $100.00-$200.00.

Lot #32. Bourjois *Glamour* clear glass bottle with gold cap, 2.5" [6.4 cm], the bottle molded with scallops, full, label on front, bottom signed *Bourjois* in the mold, in its green and white box; circa 1950's. Est. $100.00-$200.00.

Lot #33. Matchabelli *Duchess of York* and *Stradivari* clear glass bottles and gold metal stoppers, 1.4" [3.6 cm], in their pink and black hatbox. Est. $75.00-$125.00.

Lot #34. Myrurgia *Flor de Blason* clear glass bottle and metal stopper, 2.8" [7.1 cm], with pretty label, bottom marked *Myrurgia* in the mold; and matching soap, in their pretty box. Est. $150.00-$250.00.

Lot #35. Lancôme *Kypre, Flèches, Bocages, Peut-Etre* clear glass bottles and frosted stoppers, 2.3" [5.8 cm], bottom of each bottle molded *Lancôme France,* each with its label, in their pretty box. Est. $150.00-$225.00.

Lot #36. Oberon *Une Caresse,* Fragonard *Belle de Nuit, Zizanie, X mas E, Gardenia Royal, Moments Volés,* Mercoeur *Cour de France,* Lamballe *Nanette,* Carmel Myers *Gamin* clear glass bottles and gold stoppers, 1.3" [3.3 cm], in their box. Est. $100.00-$200.00.

Lot #37. Houbigant *Chantilly* clear glass miniature bottle with white cap, 2" [5.1 cm], on a pretty little chair with red cushion and flowers, in its box marked *Perfume Fantaisie.* Est. $50.00-$100.00.

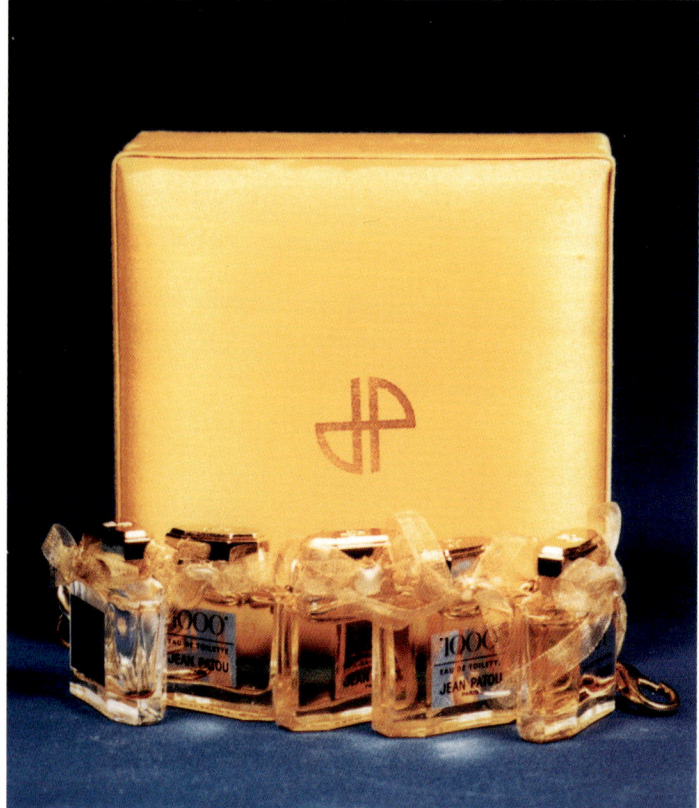

Lot #38. Jean Patou *Joy* and *1000* an interesting bracelet composed of five miniature bottles and gold stoppers, each 1.3" [3.3 cm], on a metal chain, in their beautiful yellow box. Est. $150.00-$250.00.

Lot #39. Lucien Lelong *Penthouse* set of 4 minis with gold caps, 1.6" [4 cm] each: *Whisper, Mon Image, Gardenia, Opening Night* each with tiny paper label, in their original diamond shaped box made as a sky-scraper, box height 2.5" [6.4 cm]. Est. $400.00-$500.00.

Lot #40. Bourjois *On the Wind* set of clear glass cologne bottle with orange cap, 4" [10.2 cm], and clear glass mini with orange cap, 1.7" [4.3 cm], both with pretty labels and full, in their celluloid box with original Bourjois price tag, *$1.00 plus tax.* Est. $100.00-$200.00.

Lot #41. Schiaparelli *S* tiny miniature perfume bottle and white cap, 1" [2.5 cm], held in a tiny pink and transparent plastic box. Est. $100.00-$200.00.

Lot #42. Raphael *Démon, Plaisir, Replique* clear glass bottles with glass stoppers, full and sealed, in their green carrying case. Est. $100.00-$200.00.

Lot #43. Lily Dache *Dashing* bottle shaped as a poodle sitting upright, 3.3" [8.3 cm], velvet sash with roses around waist, bottom with silver and pink label, empty. Est. $750.00-$1000.00.

Lot #44. Estée Lauder *Estée* solid perfume compact, 2" long [5.1 cm], enameled blue with a woman's portrait at center, with perfume, signed *Estée*, in its dark blue box. Est. $100.00-$175.00.

Lot #45. Estée Lauder *Youth Dew* solid perfume shaped as coiled rope with a turquoise stone at the center, label on bottom, with perfume, inside signed *Estée Lauder,* in its blue box. Est. $75.00-$150.00.

Lot #46. Guerlain *Rose du Moulin* green glass jar, 1.7" [4.3 cm], the jar bears decorative flourishes and the name *Guerlain* in gold enamel, label on bottom. This early piece is from 1907; cf. Guerlain, p. 138. Est. $125.00-$175.00.

Lot #47. Estée Lauder two different carrying cases for solid perfume, one full and one empty; Max Factor *Hypnotique,* empty, label on bottom. Three items. Est. $100.00-$150.00.

Lot #48. Estée Lauder *Beautiful* apple solid perfume, 1.2" [3.1 cm], shaped as an apple draped with the American flag, full of perfume, inside signed *Estée Lauder 2002*, with label, in in its box and outer box. Est. $200.00-$300.00.

Lot #49. Estée Lauder *Youth Dew* solid perfume, 1.8" [4.6 cm], the top mounted with a silver coin marked *Victoria Empress,* label on back, full of perfume, signed *Estee Lauder.* Est. $175.00-$250.00.

Lot #50. Estée Lauder *Estée* blue cameo solid, 1.3" x 1.7" [3.3 x 4.3 cm], the front showing a beautiful woman's head in white against blue, label on bottom, inside signed *Estée Lauter,* in its box with original price tag. Est. $125.00-$200.00.

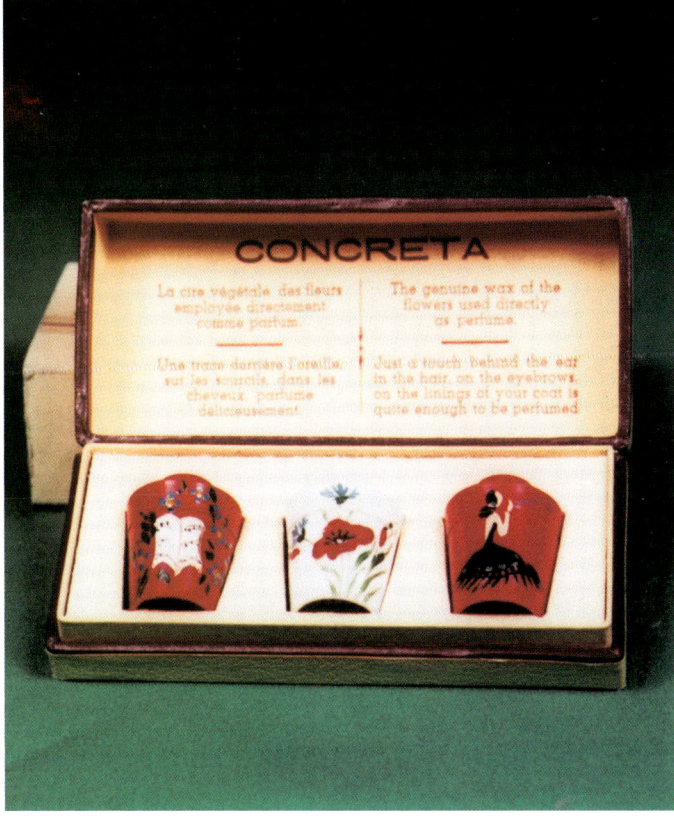

Lot #51. Estée Lauder *Youth Dew* solid perfume, 1.3" x 1.7" [3.3 x 4.3 cm], with a cameo of three ladies against an amber backround, label on back, in its box with original price tag, inside signed *Estée Lauder.* Est. $150.00-$250.00.

Lot #52. Molinard *Concreta: Iles d'Or, Habanita, Madrigal,* set of three bakelite flower pots, two red and one white, handpainted with various themes, in their original box and outer box. Est. $175.00-$250.00.

Lot #53. Estée Lauder *Youth Dew* purse necklace solid perfume, 1.3" x 1.7" [3.3 x 4.3 cm], on a long chain, empty, back with label, signed *Estee Lauder* inside. Est. $175.00-$250.00.

Lot #54. Estée Lauder *Youth Dew* solid perfume necklace, 1.6" [4.1 cm], mounted as a brooch with a dark brown stone, full of perfume, label on back, signed *Estée Lauder.* Est. $150.00-$225.00.

Lot #55. Estée Lauder *Youth Dew* cameo solid, 1.3" x 1.7" [3.3 x 4.3 cm], the front showing a beautiful woman's head in white against amber, label on bottom, inside signed *Estée Lauter,* in its box with original price tag. Est. $125.00-$200.00.

Lot #56. Helena Rubenstein *Heaven Sent* adorable perfume solid toad, 1.6" long [4.1 cm], with red jewel eyes, nearly empty of perfume, in its box. Est. $125.00-$175.00.

Lot #57. Université de Beauté *L'Étoile de la Dame de Beauté* ['The Star of the Lady of Beauty'] powder, unopened, and in its original box. Est. $100.00-$200.00.

Lot #58. Richard Hudnut *DuBarry* small compact, 1.4" x 2.2" [3.6 x 5.6 cm], empty with red powder, in its pretty pink box with tassel. Est. $75.00-$100.00.

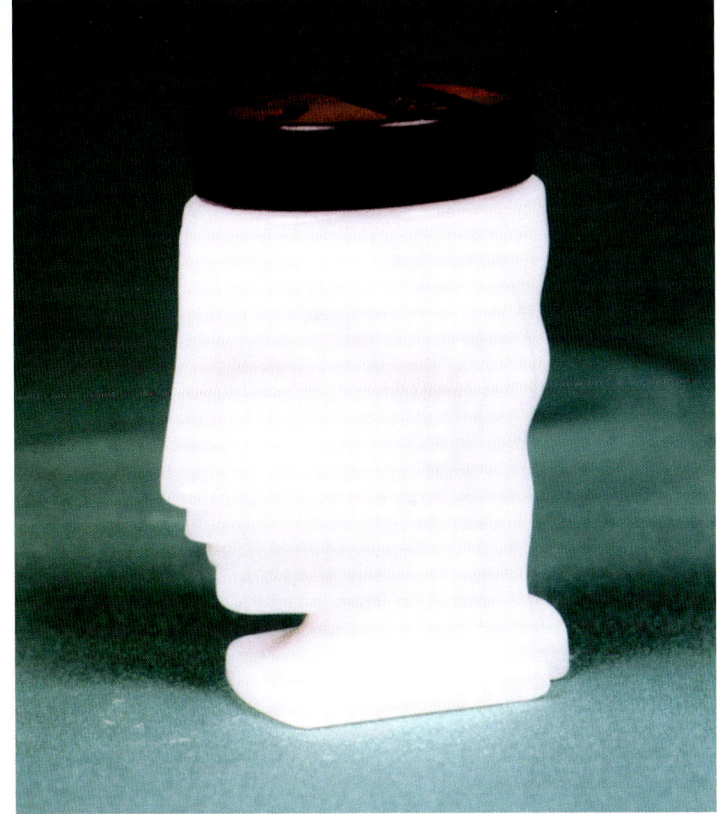

Lot #59. Sta-Nice Combination Cold and Cleansing Cream, unusual opaque white glass jar with black cap in the shape of a woman's head, 3" [7.6 cm], empty, silver, red, and black label on cap with an Art Deco graphic, bottom marked *Pat. #103910*. Est. $100.00-$150.00.

Lot #60. Molinard *Concreta Carino* [orange], *Fleurettes* [blue], *Naniko* [green], *Tabatchin* [red], *Xmas Bells* [white] set of five bakelite dice, .8" [2 cm], in their brown leather case. Est. $350.00-$450.00.

Lot #61. Ramses green glass powder dish, 3.7" [9.4 cm], of hexagonal shape, bottom marked *Ramses* in the mold. Est. $100.00-$150.00.

Lot #62. Leedall *Lavender Bath Crystals* porcelain lady in a pink dress, 5.9" [15 cm], in its original gold box. Est. $300.00-400.00.

FACTICES

Lot #63. Victoria's Secret *Encounter* clear glass bottle and ball stopper, 11.8" [30 cm], empty, names in enamel on front. Est. $150.00-$250.00.

Lot #64. Chloé clear glass bottle and frosted glass stopper with two flower-like protrusions, empty, bottom marked *HP Made in France*. Est. $100.00-$200.00.

Lot #65. Liz Claiborne *Realities* frosted glass bottle and stopper, 9.5" [24.1 cm], names in gold on front and side, bottom marked *factice*, full. Est. $100.00-$200.00.

Lot #66. Coty *Imprevu* clear glass bottle and stopper, 9.5" [24.1 cm], label in gold on front, bottom marked *Dummy*, full. Est. $150.00-$250.00.

Lot #67. Elizabeth Arden *Blue Grass* clear glass bottle with cork stopper, 12.5" [31.8 cm], with perfume, label on bottom, probably of Italian manufacture. Est. $500.00-$750.00.

Lot #68. Elizabeth Taylor *Passion for Men* deep purple glass bottle and wood cap, 11.5" [29.2 cm], molded with emanating rays, empty. Est. $100.00-$200.00.

Lot #69. D'Orsay very large size *Le Dandy* black glass bottle and stopper, 8" [20.3 cm], of octagonal pillow form with ball stopper, empty, label lacking; a very large size and probably factice. Est. $500.00-$600.00.

Lot #70. Liz Claiborne *Vivid* clear glass bottle and stopper, 14" [35.5 cm], names in enamel on front, full of blue liquid. Est. $200.00-$300.00.

Lot #71. Liz Claiborne *Lizsport* clear glass bottle and silver stopper, 14.4" [36.6 cm], full of liquid, names in enamel on front; Candie's yellow and red glass bottle and plastic top, name in silver at bottom, empty. Two items. Est. $200.00-$300.00.

Lot #72. Jean Patou *Moment Supreme* clear glass bottle and stopper, 6.3" [16 cm], with its label, bottom signed *Jean Patou France*. Est. $200.00-$300.00.

Lot #73. Elizabeth Arden *Blue Grass* display horse, 12.5" [31.8 cm], the horse on two feet and supported by a column of flowers. Est. $800.00-$1000.00.

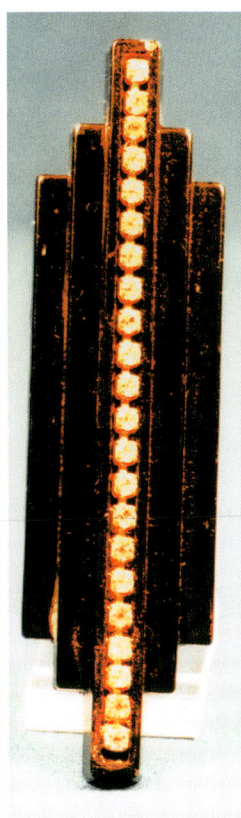

Lot #74. Drouot Richelieu catalogues for auction sale of perfume bottles, expert: Mme. Regine de Robien; November 7, 1988; May 22, 1989; May 21, 1990; November 26, 1990; December 6, 1991; May 27, 1991. Six items. Est. $300.00-$500.00.

Lot #75. Jean-Louis Scherrer black plastic pin, 4" long [10.2 cm], inset with a row of rhinestones, bottom signed *Jean-Louis Scherrer*. Est. $100.00-$150.00.

Lot #76. Drouot Richelieu catalogues for auction sale of perfume bottles, expert: Mme. Regine de Robien; December 6, 1991; May 25, 1992; April 19, 1993; December 6, 1993; October 24,1994; November 27, 1995. Six items. Est. $300.00-$500.00.

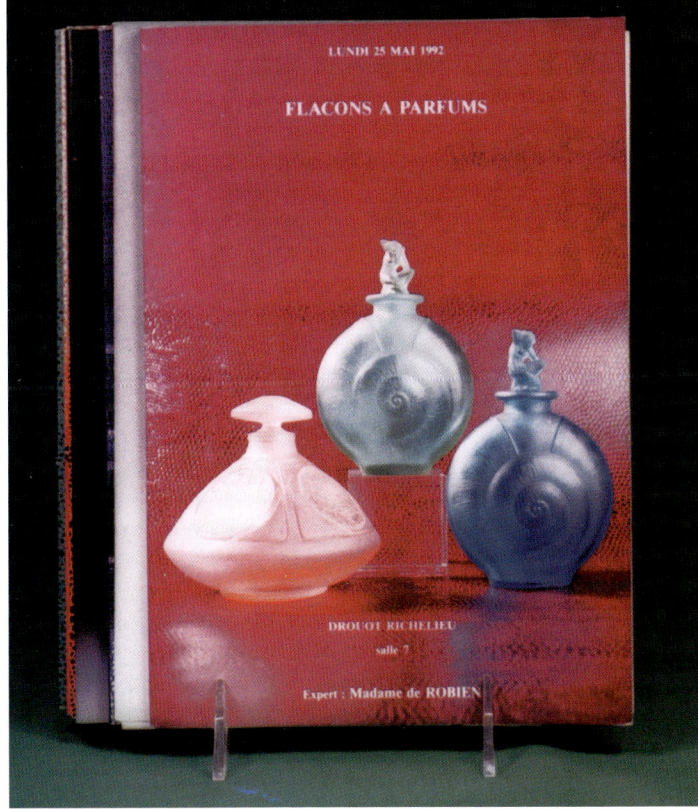

Lot #77. Drouot Richelieu catalogues for auction sale of perfume bottles, expert: Mme. Regine de Robien; November 3, 1989; November 15, 1991; December 6, 1991; May 25, 1992; October 24, 1994; June 12, 1995; June 6, 1996. Seven items. Est. $300.00-$500.00.

Lot #78. DeVilbiss trade catalogue, copyright 1926, 48 pages, all in color, one atomizer cut out, minor pencil marks, together with a color xerox copy; copy of 1930 catalogue in color Xerox form, complete; DeVibiss advertising service, 1927-28, 16 pages, together with three advertising pamphlets. Four items. Est. $400.00-$600.00.

Lot #79. *The Romance of Perfume* by Richard Le Gallienne and drawings by George Barbier together with a pamphlet entitled *At 20, Rue de la Paix,* about Richard Hudnut, 1928; a *Lanvin Perfume Portfolio*, a collection of informal talks on perfume. Two items. Est. $150.00-$250.00.

Lot #80. "Hear no Evil, See no Evil, Speak no Evil" porcelian perfume lamp, 4" tall [10.2 cm], painted in brown, gray, and pink, with the electrical apparatus but no cord, probably of German manufacture. Est. $200.00-$350.00.

Lot #81. Porcelain perfume lamp in the shape of a dog, 5.2" [13.2 cm], the young dog painted in white and brown, probably of German manufacture, newly rewired. Est. $200.00-$300.00.

Lot #82. Porcelain perfume lamp in the shape of two fish, 6.5" [16.5 cm], painted in multicolors, newly rewired. Est. $300.00-$400.00.

Lot #83. Porcelian perfume lamp in the shape of an owl, 6.7" [17 cm], the owl standing on books, original wire. Est. $300.00-$400.00.

Lot #84. Porcelian perfume lamp in the shape of an adorable puppy, 5.7" [14.5 cm], the dog sitting up, newly rewired. Est. $300.00-$400.00.

CROWN TOP AND PORCELAIN

Lot #85. Adorable perfume lamp in the shape of a cat, 6.7" [17 cm], with green eyes and sitting on a green cushion, electrical apparatus lacking, probably of German manufacture. Est. $200.00-$250.00.

Lot #86. Crown top bottle in the shape of a sphynx, 3.4" [8.6 cm], the back with the numbers *14621 Germany* impressed in the mold, with its metal crown stopper. Est. $175.00-$250.00.

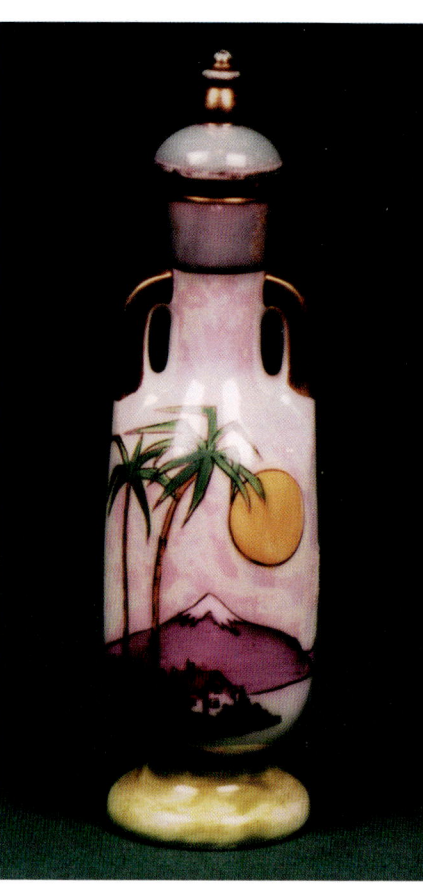

Lot #87. Porcelain crown top bottle, 4.2" [10.7 cm], in the shape of a Dutch boy holding a bouquet of flowers, bottom marked *25296*. Est. $150.00-$250.00.

Lot #88. Noritake scent bottle and stopper, 6" [15.2 cm], handpainted with a scene of a house and mountain, stopper with long glass dauber, bottom signed *Noritake*. Est. $250.00-$350.00.

Lot #89. Porcelian crown top bottle in the shape of a bird, 3.6" [9.1 cm], the front painted in blue and yellow, back marked *Germany 8639*. Est. $125.00-$175.00.

Lot #90. Crown top perfume bottle in the shape of a queen, 3.4" [8.6 cm]; crown top perfume bottle in the shape of a Dutch boy in blue and white, 3.2" [8.1 cm]; porcelain bottle of a camel with a screw on stopper, 1.8" [4.6 cm]. Three items. Est. $200.00-$300.00.

Lot #91. German porcelain perfume bottle in the shape of a Pierrot holding an urn of flowers, 4.9" [12.5 cm], the stopper of pink flowers having a long glass dauber, bottom signed *Bavaria*. Est. $300.00-$400.00.

DECORATIVE - VICTORIAN BOTTLES

Lot #92. Five items: red glass bottle, decorated with white leaves, 4" [10.2 cm]; clear glass bottle with gold decoration, 3.2" [8.1 cm]; clear glass bottle with gold decor, 3.7" [9.4 cm]; clear and green glass bottle and metal stopper, 3.3" [8.4 cm]; clear glass bottle with sterling top, marked *Birmingham, 1924*. Five items. Est. $200.00-$300.00.

Lot #93. Clear glass dish with sterliing silver and tortoise top, British hallmarks; dish with sterling silver top, hallmarked *Birmingham 1890*; green crystal covered dish, marked *Czechoslovakia;* two additional dishes with sterling silver tops. Five items. Est. $200.00-$300.00.

Lot #94. Three bottle set: clear glass bottles with inner glass stoppers and metal overcaps, 2.6" [6.6 cm], the caps enameled green, red, and blue, in their brown leather traveling case. Est. $100.00-$150.00.

Lot #95. Black and green crystal bottle, 6.4" [16.3 cm], with neat symmetrical lines, possibly of Czechoslovakian manufacture. Est. $150.00-$250.00.

Lot #96. Clear glass bottle and frosted glass stopper, 7.5" [19 cm], the stopper formed as a nude sitting atop a ball, very heavy ball shaped base, unmarked. Est. $300.00-$400.00.

Lot #97. Gigantic glass bottle encased in a metal framework, 10.5" [26.7 cm], the perfume contained in a small interior container, stopper with long dauber, unsigned. Est. $100.00-$200.00.

Lot #98. Pretty bottle with a hummingbird stopper, 9" [22.9 cm], the perfume well of rose colored glass, unmarked. Est. $100.00-$150.00.

Lot #99. Heavy crystal bottle and stopper with dauber, 7.9" [20 cm], the central panel with a gold seal marked *Dieu et Les Dames* ['God and the Women'], bottom unmarked. Est. $75.00-$125.00.

Lot #100. Sabino clear glass bottle and stopper, 6.7" [17 cm], the bottle an abstract geometric form, the stopper impressed with a basket of flowers, bottom signed *France*. Est. $150.00-$300.00.

Lot #101. Royal Copenhagen porcelain scent bottle and stopper, 4.8" [12.2 cm], molded with a nude with hands aloft, the reverse with a flying goose, bottom with paper label and marked number *4015*. Est. $100.00-$200.00.

Lot #102. Pressed glass dish and cover, 5.4" [13.7 cm], the cover mounted with the figure of a mule trudging slowly, unmarked but probably of American manufacture. Est. $40.00-$75.00.

Lot #103. Ladies compact, 3.5" [8.9 cm] exclusive of chain, beautifully enameled in blue with pink and blue flowers, containing tiny lipstick and powder holder [empty] and a mirror, on a chain with ring. Est. $400.00-$500.00.

Lot #104. Clear glass bottles with inner stoppers and metal overcaps, 2" [5.1 cm], held in their very old trunk, country of origin undetermined. Est. $150.00-$250.00.

Lot #105. Early twentieth century French miniature bottles and cork stoppers, each 2.2" [5.6 cm], held in place by a metal framework and an early picture of the Arch de Triomphe in Paris. Est. $150.00-$250.00.

Lot #106. Interesting bottle shaped as a nut with silver top, 2.1" [5.3 cm]; ivory or bone bottle, stopper molded as a bouquet of flowers, 3.5" [8.9 cm]; shell bottle with a metal back, 2.2" [5.5 cm]. Three items. Est. $150.00-$250.00.

Lot #107. Porcelain bottle covered in old red cloth, 2.4" [6.1 cm]; bottle shaped as a shell, with metal cap, 2.5" [6.4 cm], chips to shell; bottle made of a tiny clam shell, with a metal medallion, 1.6" [4.1 cm]. Three items. Est. $150.00-$250.00.

Lot #108. Metal and mother of pearl bottle shaped as a ewer, 2.6" [6.6 cm]; tiny glass bottle with metal on both sides and a cork stopper, 1.9" [4.8 cm]; glass bottle marked *Africa* covered in tiny beads and with cork stopper, 2.5" [6.4 cm]. Three items. Est. $100.00-$200.00.

Lot #109. Silver topped perfume bottle, cut with flowers on six sides, top with hallmarks for *Birmingham, 1940*, 5" [12.7 cm]; cut crystal bottle with silver top 3.2" [8.2 cm]; cut glass perfume bottle with silver top, hallmarks for *Birmingham, 1946*. Three items. Est. $400.00-$550.00.

Lot #110. Lot of 6: two cut glass column bottles, 2.6" [6.6 cm]; round bottle with silver top, 2.5" [6.4 cm]; bottle with sterling silver top, 2.1" [5.3 cm], hallmarked *Birmingham, 1926;* cut glass pin dish; glass bottle with silver top, 2.6" [6.6 cm]. Six items. Est. $150.00-$250.00.

Lot #111. Lot of three 'lavender' bottles, the tallest 7.6" [19.3 cm], decorated with gold and white enamel and with different designs in the glass. Est. $150.00-$250.00.

Lot #112. Beautiful massive bottle and stopper, 6" [15.2 cm], both bottle and stopper inset with millefiori of blue, yellow, and red, country of origin undetermined. Est. $200.00-$300.00.

Lot #113. Lot of three 'lavender' bottles: 6.5", 6.1", and 4.1" [16.5 to 10.4 cm], decorated differently with gold and white enamel. Three items. Est. $100.00-$200.00.

Lot #114. Beautiful bottle shaped as an egg of stone, cork lined stopper, 1.6" [4.1 cm]; delicate ivory bottle shaped as an egg with snifter inside; wood bottle shaped as an egg with snifter inside. Three items. Est. $400.00-$600.00.

Lot #115. Clear crystal bottle and inner glass stopper and silver metal overcap, 3.6" [9.1 cm], cut on both sides with a pretty floral design in yellow glass, probably of Bohemian manufacture. Est. $150.00-$250.00.

Lot #116. White porcelain scent bottle, 3.3" [8.4 cm], decorated with the heads of two angels on the sides; yellow porcelian scent bottle, 4.8" [12.2 cm], the bottle broken and glued; tiny porcelain bottle with a man serenading a woman, top lacking, 1.1" [2.8 cm]. Three items. Est. $100.00-$200.00.

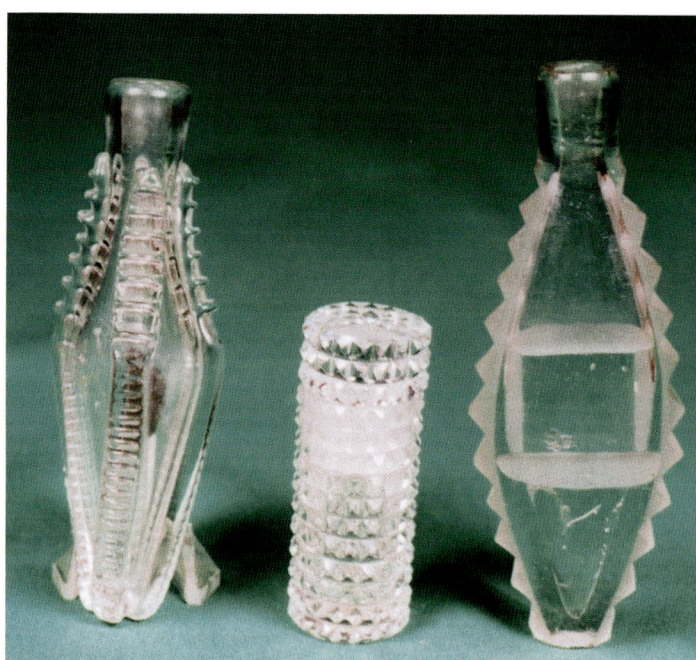

Lot #117. Very old glass bottle, 4.2" [10.7 cm], sides frosted; glass bottle decorated with four glass bands, 3.9" [9.9 cm], crystal bottle and screw on stopper, 2.2" [5.6 cm]. Three items. Est. $150.00-$250.00.

Lot #118. Red and clear glass bottle and stopper with silver metal overcap, 1.6" [4.1 cm], the bottle cut with lines and with a star on the bottom. Est. $150.00-$250.00.

Lot #119. Clear glass bottles and stoppers overlaid with silver, 2.5" and 2.9" [6.4 and 7.4 cm], country of origin undetermined. Two items. Est. $200.00-$300.00.

Lot #120. Royal Crown Derby double scent bottle, highly decorated with flowers and leaves, full crown mark on base, 1877-9; two very old perfume flasks, one possibly ancient. Three items. Est. $300.00-$450.00.

Lot #121. Blue glass bottle and clear glass stopper and metal overcap, 2" [5.1 cm], beautifully painted with gold flowers and leaves, inscribed with the word *Venise*, French for Venice. Est. $150.00-$250.00.

Lot #122. Green glass bottle and stopper, 3.7" [9.4 cm], encased in a silver design, the tongue of stopper with a chip. Est. $100.00-$200.00.

Lot #123. Molded early plastic bottle and screw-on stopper, 3" [7.6 cm], molded on both sides with a maiden's head and many flowers and leaves, country of origin unidentified. Est. $100.00-$200.00.

Lot #124. Three Dutch Schoonhoven clear crystal bottles with silver tops and plinths, two with glass inner stoppers, one hallmarked with a dagger. Est. $350.00-$450.00.

Lot #125. Two cut glass bottle and prism stoppers, 4.5" [11.4 cm], a star motif cut into the bottles on four sides, bottom also with star motif. Two items. Est. $150.00-$250.00.

Lot #126. Clear glass bottle and stopper, 6.6" [16.8 cm], minor chips to stopper; clear glass bottle encased in metal with metal stopper, 6.5" [16.5 cm]; clear glass bottle and stopper with chips, 6.2" [15.7 cm]. Three items. Est. $100.00-$200.00.

Lot #127. Porcelain scent bottle with a blue design, 4" [10.2 cm], possibly of Danish manufacture; porcelain bottle with silver top, 2.1" [5.3 cm], painted with a couple; circular bottle with gold decor, 2.5" [6.4 cm]. Three items. Est. $250.00-$350.00.

Lot #128. Lot of 9 perfume pins: of various heights, some marked *Austria*, some of green glass, some clear, some adorned with jewels. Nine items. Est. $400.00-$500.00.

Lot #129. Red glass bottle, 2.4" [6.1 cm], painted in white enamel; clear bottle with silver top and ring, 2.5" [6.4 cm]; frosted bottle with inner stopper and metal overcap, 1.7" [4.3 cm], with chain. Three items. Est. $100.00-$200.00.

Lot #130. Porcelain scent bottle and cap, 4.6" [11.7 cm], painted with an oriental scene; porcelain scent bottle with crown top, 3" [7.6 cm], handpainted with flowers; porcelain bottle handpained with lines in various colors, 2.5" [6.4 cm]. Three items. Est. $150.00-$250.00.

Lot #131. Silver overlay bottle, 2.5" [6.4 cm]; two silver overlay bottles, 2.5" [6.4 cm]; one bottle shaped as an acorn, with a metal cover, 1.5" [3.8 cm]. Four items. Est. $100.00-$200.00.

Lot #132. Lot of two very old earthen bottles, 3.5" [8.9 cm], identical shape, age undetermined, but these are possibly very old. Est. $100.00-$200.00.

Lot #133. Cut glass bottle with inner stopper and sterling overcap, hallmarked *Birmingham, 1912;* glass bottle with inner stopper and metal overcap, 3.5" [8.9 cm], wheel cut with a beautiful tropical scene; glass bottle with inner stopper and gold metal cap, 2.8" [7.1 cm]. Three items. Est. $250.00-$350.00.

Lot #134. Lot of three silver perfume objects: urn, whose top and bottom open, hallmarks on bottom, 3.5" [8.9 cm]; three footed urn, maker's mark on bottom, 3.2" [8.1 cm]; Japanese top-opening vinaigrette bucket, with a scene around it, 2.1" [5.3 cm]. Three items. Est. $200.00-$300.00.

Lot #136. Porcelain scent bottle with silver top, 3.1" [7.8 cm], handpainted with a fanciful design of flowers, neck of bottle marked *Sterling Birmingham, 1893.* Est. $125.00-$200.00.

Lot #135. Beautiful turquoise glass bottle with applied decor and metal stopper, 5.5" [14 cm]; light green glass bottle, 4" [10.2 cm], stopper frozen; blue, clear, and white glass bottle and stopper, 2.8" [7.1 cm]. Three items. Est. $200.00-$300.00.

Lot #137. Crystal bottle with carved design of a cupid in a charriot, 4.6" [11.17 cm]; porcelain bottle handpainted with a design of a lake and flowers, 4.2" [10.7 cm]; porcelain scent bottle handpainted with a floral decor, 2.9" [7.4 cm]. Three items. Est. $400.00-$500.00.

Lot #138. Pretty white glass bottle with inner glass stopper and metal overcap, 2.8" [7.1 cm], decorated with red enamel flowers and leaves. Est. $200.00-$300.00.

Lot #139. Tiny clear glass bottle with silver cap, 1.5" [3.8 cm], cut with squares; red glass bottle with inner glass stopper and brass metal overcap, 2.2" [5.6 cm], painted with golden flowers. Two items. Est. $200.00-$300.00.

Lot #140. Lot of three silver vinaigrettes: one, .8" [2 cm], with elaborate design all over; tiny globe which unscrews in the middle, .6" [1.5 cm]; metal pineapple whose top unscrews, 1.6" [4 cm]. Three items. Est. $700.00-$900.00.

Lot #141. Beautiful opaque glass scent bottle with a decor of leaves, 5.2" [13.2 cm], glass stopper and silver cap with hallmarks for *London, 1903*; opaque white glass bottle and stopper, 3.2" [8.3 cm]; porcelain handpainted bottle, no stopper, 2.4" [6.1 cm]; porcelain honeycomb bottle with a green bee on both sides, 4.1" [10.4 cm]. Four items. Est. $400.00-$600.00.

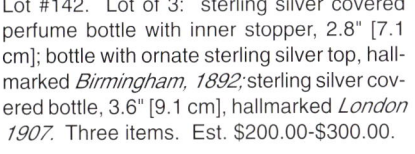

Lot #142. Lot of 3: sterling silver covered perfume bottle with inner stopper, 2.8" [7.1 cm]; bottle with ornate sterling silver top, hall-marked *Birmingham, 1892;* sterling silver covered bottle, 3.6" [9.1 cm], hallmarked *London 1907.* Three items. Est. $200.00-$300.00.

Lot #143. Silver flask shaped bottle with a bird design, 2.6" [6.6 cm]; silver bottle and stopper with a metal pick at the side, 3.4" [8.6 cm]; silver hinged box with two birds atop, 2.7" [6.9 cm]; silver bottle shaped as a mandolin, one key lacking, makers mark at top. Four items. Est. $600.00-$750.00.

Lot #144. Clear glass bottle and stopper, 5.5" [14 cm], both bottle and stopper inset with millefiori glass, stopper with long dauber, country of origin undetermined. Est. $150.00-$250.00.

Lot #145. Turquoise glass bottle and inner glass stopper with metal overcap, 2.9" [7.4 cm], the front of the bottle painted with a scroll-like effect, on a chain with ring, back marked *Czechoslovakia* with paper label and also *Hall House, New York*. Est. $250.00-$350.00.

Lot #146. Light blue glass bottle and brass metal overcap, 4.7" [12 cm], inner stopper lacking, on a metal base. Est. $100.00-$200.00.

Lot #147. Yellow amber glass perfume bottle and inner glass stopper and metal overcap, 3.9" [9.9 cm], the bottle cut with a star like motif, probably of continental manufacture. Est. $200.00-$300.00.

Lot #148. Beautiful crystal bottle and stopper with metal neck and chain, 3.1" [7.8 cm], the bottle of flat egg shape. Est. $150.00-$250.00.

Lot #149. Yellow porcelian bottle and stopper, 3.1" [7.8 cm], the front painted with roses, stopper with its long dauber, bottom marked *Dresden Saxony.* Est. $100.00-$175.00.

Lot #150. Red glass scent bottle with sterling neck, 3.8" [9.6 cm], probably of French manufacture, circa 1850-1860. Est. $500.00-$750.00.

Lot #151. Beautiful quality green glass bottle and stopper, 5" [12.7 cm], handpainted with decorative bands of gold chains, unmarked. Est. $300.00-$400.00.

Lot #152. Webb scent bottle with glass stopper and sterling silver cap, 4.4" [11.2 cm], the bottle of red glass overlaid with white, carved on both sides, unsigned. Est. $1,800.00-$2,500.00.

Lot #153. Lot of 4: Clear glass bottle, inner stopper, and sterling silver overcap marked *Tchecoslovaquie;* clear glass bottle, inner stopper and overcap, marked *Sterling, Birmingham, 1942;* opalescent green glass bottle and silver cover, inscribed with flowers; cut glass bottle with silver top enameled with a lady in red. Four items. Est. $300.00-$400.00.

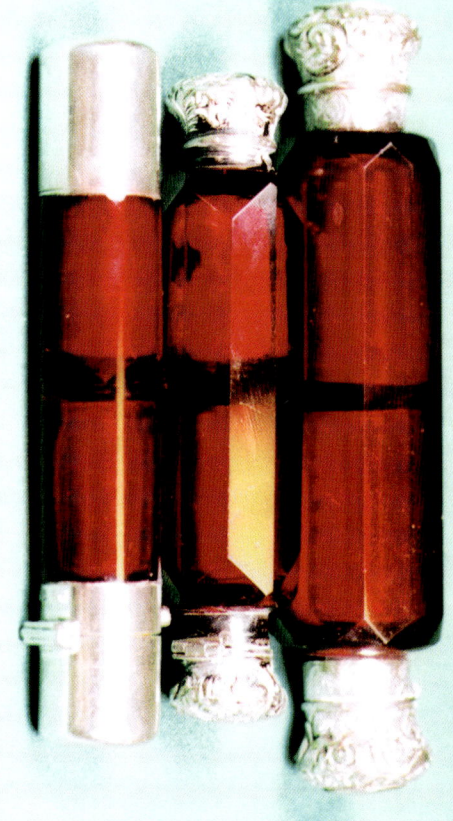

Lot #154. Dark green crystal bottle and inner glass stopper and metal overcap, 2.5" [6.4 cm], bearing the hallmarks for *Birmingham, England, 1892.* Est. $150.00-$250.00.

Lot #155. Red crystal bottle with silver caps, 5" [12.7 cm], internal bruise on one side; clear crystal bottle and silver caps with hallmarks, 5" [12.7 cm]; red crystal bottle with sterling silver caps, 4" [10.2 cm], hallmarked *London 1944;* red bottle with silver caps, 3.9" [9.9 cm]; clear glass bottle with silver cap, 3.3" [8.4 cm]. Five items. Est. $300.00-$500.00.

Lot #156. Beautiful and large perfume bottle and stopper, 7" [17.8 cm], composed of three layers of glass: blue over white over clear, and cut back to expose one or more colors, unmarked. Est. $800.00-$1,000.00.

Lot #157. Beautiful bottle of blue over clear glass with conforming stopper, 5.9" [15 cm], the four sided bottle cut-back with four huge medallions of blue glass and decorated in gold, star motif in bottom. Est. $200.00-$300.00.

Lot #158. Beautiful quality Victorian bottle of clear and red glass, 5.8" [14.7 cm], decorated in cream and gold, unsigned, of English manufacture. Est. $300.00-$400.00.

Lot #159. Beautiful etched bottle and stopper covered in silver, 5" [12.7 cm], the bottle covered with an etched design, neck of the bottle and bottom part in silver, continental silver marks on bottom. Est. $300.00-$400.00.

Lot #160. Clear glass bottle and inner stopper with sterling silver neck and overcap, 2.9" [7.4 cm], the stopper enameled with a design in blue enamel, signed with sterling hallmarks for *Birmingham, 1927*. Est. $150.00-$250.00.

Lot #161. Clear glass bottle and stopper, 5.5" [14 cm], the heavy base highly cut, stopper with many facets, unsigned. Est. $150.00-$250.00.

Lot #162. Limoges enamel-over-copper scent bottle with inner glass stopper and overcap, 2.5" [6.4 cm], showing a lady in a beautiful turquoise dress against a red background. Est. $650.00-$850.00.

Lot #163. Clear cut glass bottle and stopper, 5" [12.7 cm], the bottle highly cut including on base, faceted ball stopper, unsigned. Est. $150.00-$250.00.

Lot #164. Wonderful tiny crystal bottle and stopper with glass inner stopper, 1.6" [4.1 cm], in an egg-shaped carrying case made of mother of pearl. Est. $200.00-$300.00.

Lot #165. Clear glass bottle which fades to vaseline color and its sterling silver top, 8" [20.3 cm], hallmarked *Birmingham, England, circa 1897.* Est. $450.00-$650.00.

Lot #166. Opaque white glass bottle and stopper, 6.2" [15.7 cm], with inner stopper and cap set with many stones, two cupids hanging from either side, unmarked. Est. $400.00-$500.00.

Lot #167. Clear glass bottle and metal stopper, 4.5" [11.4 cm], all four sides of the bottle with a colored scene, stopper impressed with a metal image of George III, king at the time of the American Revolution. Est. $400.00-$500.00.

Lot #168. Webb teal blue scent bottle with metal stopper, 3.3" [8.4 cm], overalid with white glass, tiny restoration to neck of bottle, the Webb butterfly on the reverse side. Est. $1,000.00-$1,250.00.

Lot #169. Unusual Victorian clear glass bottle of barrel shape, total height 4.3" [10.1 cm] including metal frame, decorated with red and turquoise stones. Est. $300.00-$400.00.

Lot #170. Red cut back to clear bottle and sterling silver neck and cover, 5" [12.7 cm], the bottle elaborately cut in a pattern, bottle neck with hallmarks for *Birmingham 1938*. Est. $150.00-$250.00.

Lot #171. French red enamelled perfume bottle, inner stopper, and overcap, 3" [7.6 cm], a beautiful design of red, white, and gold in perfect condition, with silver mountings, unsigned. Est. $1,000.00-$1,200.00.

Lot #172. Webb cameo glass bottle of white over avocado green, 5" [12.7 cm], with a design of lilies, Webb butterfly on the back, sterling silver hall-marked *Birmingham, circa 1887.* Est. $2,500.00-$3,000.00.

Lot #173. French gold over crystal scent bottle with inner stopper and overcap, 4.6" [11.7 cm], the top with a cabachon garnet top, with original gold and cork stopper, circa 1860-1880. Est. $3,000.00-$3,500.00.

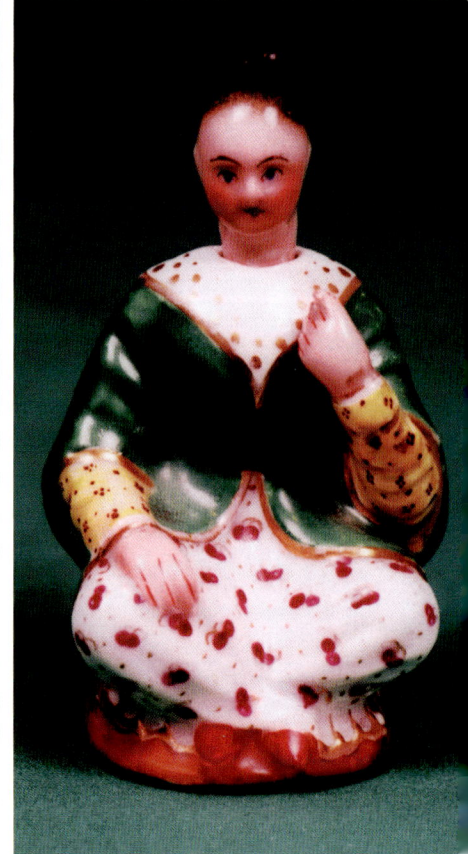

Lot #174. Magnificent English porcelain bottle shaped as a man with flowers, 3.4" [8.6 cm], his fancy outfit decorated with bows and painted in multicolors, bottom with a gold anchor mark. Est. $2,000.00-$2,500.00.

Lot #175. Black glass bottle mounted on a metal stand, 5.5" [14 cm], the bottle beautifully painted in white enamel with flowers, country of origin undetermined. Est. $100.00-$200.00.

Lot #176. Beautifully painted oriental man, 3" [7.6 cm], with a green and white robe, various marks on the bottom including the letter *S*, probably of English manufacture. Est. $800.00-$1200.00.

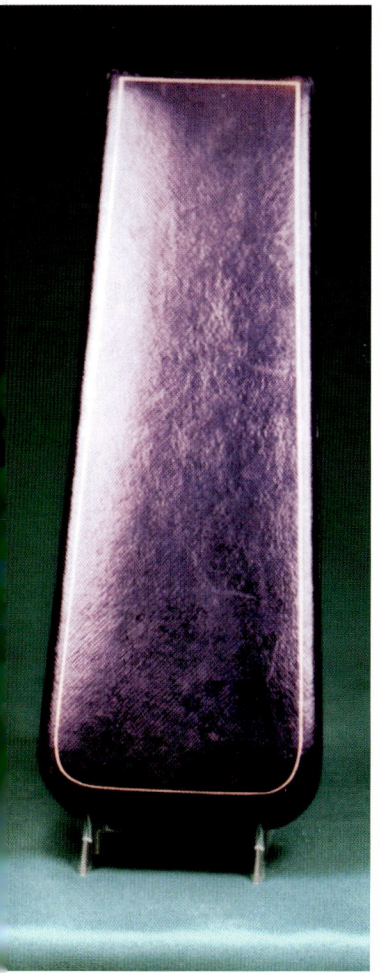

Lot #177. Beautiful perfume flacon and lipstick, perfume 3" [7.6 cm], on a violet cord and tassel; the lipstick, in unused condition, is concealed by the tassel, in it original box. Est. $2,000.00-$2,500.00.

Lot #178. Beautiful clear glass bottle and metal atomizer attachment, 6" [15.2 cm], the bottle highly cut, new ball, unsigned. Est. $200.00-$300.00.

Lot #179. Pink glass bottle with geometric decoration on a metal atomizer stand, 4.7" [12 cm], bottom marked *Foreign*. Est. $200.00-$300.00.

Lot #180. Clear glass botte and metal atomizer, 2.6" wide [6.6 cm]; decorated with stylized flowers on the four corners, unsigned. Est. $100.00-$200.00.

Lot #181. Pink glass atomizer bottle decorated with gold enamel, 6.9" [17.5 cm], original atomizer ball, unsigned. Est. $150.00-$250.00.

Lot #182. Cased glass perfume bottle decorated with a frieze of nude cupids, 6.7" [17 cm], internally enameled in orange, new ball and tassel, atomizer stamped *Made in France*. Est. $200.00-$300.00.

Lot #183. Pink glass atomizer bottle with a stepped motif, 6.9" [17.5 cm], original atomizer ball, unsigned. Est. $200.00-$300.00.

Lot #184. Clear crystal bottle and atomizer attachment, 7.3" [18.5 cm], the bottle cut with a floral design on four sides, atomizer neck signed *DeVilbiss*. Est. $150.00-$250.00.

Lot #185. Clear and frosted glass bottle and metal atomizer, 7.4" [18.8 cm], the three sided bottle with geometric motifs in clear and frosted glass and with gold lining, original atomizer ball, marked *Made in France for Saks Fifth Avenue*. Est. $200.00-$300.00.

Lot #186. Enormous atomizer of glass with metal atomizer top, 9.5" [24.1 cm], the perfume well enameled in black and gold, unsigned, pink atomizer ball and tassel. Est. $400.00-$500.00.

Lot 187.   Dark red over yellow glass bottle with metal atomizer top, 7" [17.8 cm], neck impressed *Czechoslovakia* and bottom with paper label, atomizer ball lacking. Est. $100.00-$200.00.

Lot #188.   Unidentified clear glass bottle with gold enamel, 7.3" [18.5 cm], of beautiful design, unsigned. Est. $200.00-$300.00.

Lot #189.   Volupté rare decorated glass bottle with metal atomizer, 9.3" [23.6 cm], internally enameled in green and decorated with Jazz age motifs, unsigned. Est. $1,500.00-$2,000.00.

Lot #190.   Pyramid beautiful pair of black glass bottles, one with atomizer attachment and one with its long glass dauber, new atomizer ball, decorated with a band of flowers in gold, both with their gold and black Pyramid labels. Est. $500.00-$750.00.

Lot #191.   Sumptuous atomizer on an elaborate metal and glass holder, total height 7.5" [19 cm], the crystal bottle cut and partially frosted and enameled in black, atomizer ball lacking, unsigned. Est. $1,750.00-$2,250.00.

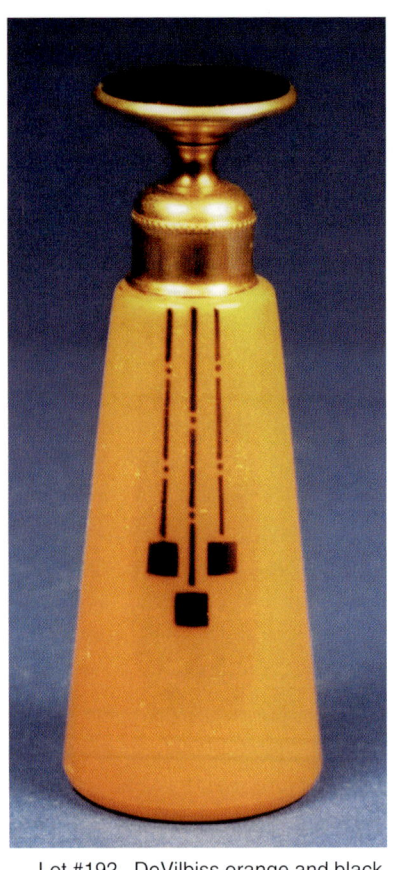

Lot #192. DeVilbiss orange and black enameled bottle, 4.7" [12 cm], stopper with long dauber, original DeVilbiss label on the side. Est. $150.00-$200.00.

Lot #193. Green glass bottle with metal atomizer, 7" [17.8 cm], cut back to clear on oval panels and handpainted with flowers, unsigned. Est. $100.00-$200.00.

Lot #194. Marcel Franck two glass atomizers, 5.5" [14 cm], of gently sloping form, both signed *Marcel Franck France* at the neck. Two items. Est. $100.00-$175.00.

Lot #195. DeVilbiss pink perfume bottle and dropper, 4.2" [10.7 cm], of octagonal shape with the edges outlined in gold, with its dauber, unsigned. Est. $150.00-$250.00.

Lot #196. DeVilbiss light translucent amber bottle with metal atomizer, 6.5" [16.5 cm], the bottle of baluster form and delicately molded with smooth vertical ribs, new atomizer ball and tassel, bottom signed *DeVilbiss* in gold. Est. $300.00-$400.00.

Lot #197. Frosted glass dropper bottle enameled in green, 4.6" [11.7 cm], stopper with long dauber, decorated with three panels of flowers, with original DeVilbiss tag marked *DE 19*, bottom signed *DeVilbiss*. Est. $200.00-$300.00.

Lot #198. DeVilbiss rare lavender glass perfume atomizer, 6.7" [17 cm], the base decorated with a band of leaves in gold, original atomizer ball, original DeVibiss label on base. Est. $600.00-$750.00.

Lot #199. DeVilbiss red glass bottle and metal atomizer top, 7.4" [18.8 cm], the bottle beautifully etched with a design of curls in gold, bottom signed *DeVilbiss*. Est. $450.00-$600.00.

Lot #200. Black glass perfume bottle with original atomizer attachment, 6.8" [17.3 cm], the black glass infused with gold in an abstract pattern, black DeVilbiss label on base, bottom signed *DeVilbiss*. Est. $300.00-$400.00.

Lot #201. DeVilbiss light amber glass ginger jar and cover with atomizer insert [bruise to glass well], 6.3" [16 cm], etched with a pine needle design and enameled in gold, apparently unsigned. DeV #S800-6 [1937]. Est. $500.00-$650.00.

Lot #202. Light amber glass bottle with metal atomizer and acorn finial, 10.3" [26.1 cm], the lower part etched with an elaborate scroll design and enameled in gold, original ball, bottom signed *DeVilbiss* in gold enamel. Est. $800.00-$1,000.00.

Lot #203. DeVilbiss perfume lamp with carved ship, 6.3" [16 cm], the ship being tossed in high seas, small dove in the foreground, perfume well lacking, electrified. Est. $400.00-$500.00.

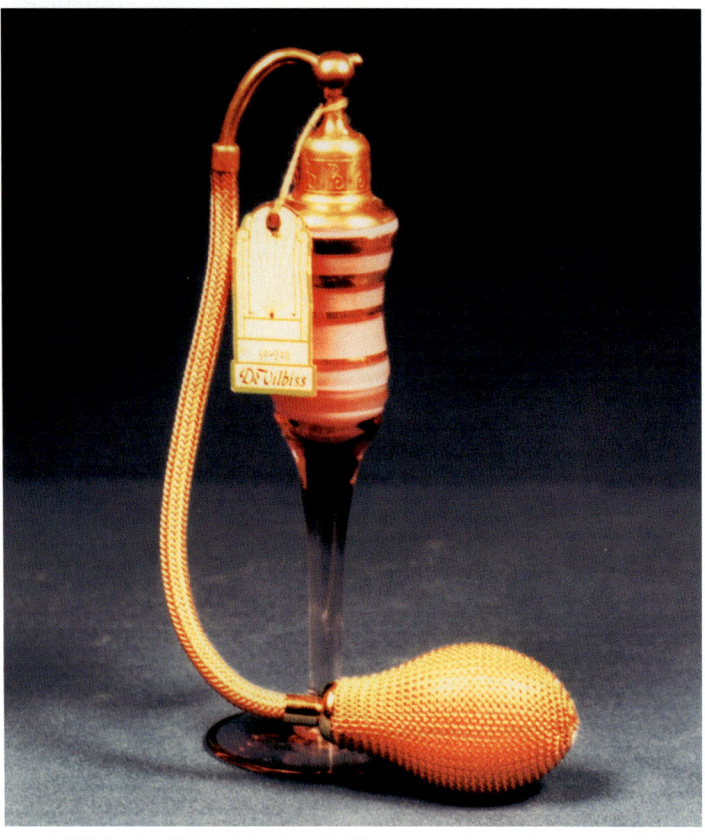

Lot #204. DeVilbiss pink glass bottle and metal atomizer top, 6.5" [16.5 cm], the bottle decorated with gold bands, with original DeVilbiss tag marked *SP-240,* new ball, unsigned. Est. $200.00-$275.00.

Lot #205. Amber glass bottle with glass dauber, 6" [15.2 cm], bottom signed *DeVilbiss;* clear glass bottle with metal atomizer top [original but hardened ball], bottom with DeVilbiss label marked *S350-45.* Two items. Est. $175.00-$250.00.

Lot #206. Fine quality DeVilbiss caramel color perfume bottle, 6.2" [15.7 cm], stopper enameled black and gold, bottom etched *DeVilbiss,* in its presentation case with DeVilbiss sticker. Est. $600.00-$750.00.

Lot #207. DeVilbiss perfume lamp, 7.5" [19 cm], the white glass column reverse-painted in orange and decorated with dancing women with its well, and electrified, unsigned. Est. $400.00-$500.00.

Lot #208. DeVilbiss perfume atomizer, 6.8" [17.3 cm], enameled in gold and hand painted with flowers and leaves, signed *DeVilbiss.* Est. $300.00-$400.00.

Lot #209. Beautiful amber glass atomizer and dropper bottles, 7" tall [17.8 cm], the amber glass internally enameled in black, an abstract gold design on the exterior, bottom of one signed *DeVilbiss*. Est. $400.00-$500.00.

Lot #210. Clear glass perfume bottles, 7" [17.8 cm] and 6.2" [15.7 cm], a transparent window around the top, in gold and black, original [hardened] atomizer ball, both signed *DeVilbiss* in gold. Est. $400.00-$600.00.

Lot #211. DeVilbiss statuesque clear glass bottle with gold acorn finial, 9.8" [24.9 cm], wheel-cut with birds and flowers, with gold enamel, new ball, unsigned. Est. $750.00-$1,000.00.

Lot #212. Enormous amber glass atomizer, 10.2" [26 cm], the base decorated with multicolored flowers, atomizer bulb lacking, bottom faintly signed *DeVilbiss*. Est. $400.00-$600.00.

Lot #213. DeVilbiss glass bottle with atomizer, 10" [25.4 cm], decorated with red translucent and gold enamel, black acorn stopper, new atomizer ball, signed *DeVilbiss*. Est. $750.00-$1,000.00.

53

Lot #214. DeVilbiss set of powder jar and perfume atomizer, 3.7" tall [9.4 cm], unused condition, both decorated with abstract motifs, bottom of perfume signed *DeVilbiss*, in its original box. Est. $350.00-$450.00.

Lot #215. DeVilbiss rare purse atomizer of brass and green bakelite, 1.9" [4.8 cm], a unique design, in its original box signed *DeVilbiss*. DeV #G-99 [1930]. Est. $300.00-$500.00.

ART GLASS - CRYSTAL NANCY - DAUM - BACCARAT

Lot #216. DeVilbiss powder jar, 3" [7.6 cm], entirely enameled in gold and with handpainted flowers on the lid, unsigned. Est. $100.00-$200.00.

Lot #217. Guerlain *Coque d'Or* ['Bow of Gold'] cobalt blue glass bottle and stopper, 2.5" [6.4 cm], in the form of a bowtie, covered in gold enamel, names in black enamel on either side, empty, probably unsigned. Bacc. #770 [1937]. Est. $500.00-$750.00.

Lot #218. Caron *Les Pois de Senteur de Chez Moi* ['My Very Own Sweet Peas'], clear crystal bottle and stopper, 6" [15.2 cm], label soiled, empty, with Baccarat emblem on bottom. Bacc. #809 [1947]. Est. $150.00-$250.00.

Lot #219. Guerlain *Jicky*, 2.5" [6.4 cm], full and sealed, in its box with Mexican tax stamp [not Baccarat]; *Rue de la Paix* clear crystal bottle and stopper, 3.8" [9.6 cm], with perfume, with label, bottom signed *Baccarat* in emblem. Bacc. #24 [1908/1947]. Est. $250.00-$400.00.

Lot #220. Guerlain *L'Heure Bleue* clear crystal bottle and stopper of inverted heart shape, 4.8" [11.5 cm], mounted with an elaborate metal framework featuring a woman's head on both sides, marked *Crystal Nancy.* Bacc. ref. #171 [1947]. Est. $100.00-$200.00.

Lot #221. Fioret *Les Jardins de Fioret* ['The Gardens of Fioret'], clear crystal bottle with brass cap, 2.2" [5.6 cm], empty, inner stopper lacking, in its leather pouch with the names impressed into the leather; metal cap signed *Fioret Paris*. Bacc. #543 [1924]. Est. $125.00-$225.00.

Lot #222. L. T. Piver *Floramye Concentré* clear crystal bottle and stopper with long dauber, 2.4" [6.1 cm], as a cigarette lighter, names on front, signed *Baccarat* in emblem. Bacc. #411 [1919]. Est. $400.00-$600.00.

Lot #223. D'Orsay *Jasmin* clear crystal bottle and stopper, 2.4" [6 cm], of circular form, with its label, and a half of an old Baccarat label, in its original black pouch, signed *D'Orsay.* Est. $250.00-$350.00.

Lot #224. Lubin *L'Ocean Bleu* rare clear crystal bottle and stopper, 6.1" [15.5 cm], as two dolphins, empty, signed *Baccarat;* the original of this was for the *1925 Exposition des Arts Decoratifs* in Paris. Est. $800.00-$1,000.00.

Lot #225. Daum light green and violet bottle and stopper, 4.7" [11.9 cm], the stopper molded as an iris, the bottle with leaves all around, bottom signed *Daum,* in its original box. Est. $350.00-$450.00.

Lot #226. Bourjois *Miss Kate* clear glass bottle and black glass stopper, 4.6" [11.7 cm], of urn shape, bottom marked *St. Louis France.* Est. $400.00-$500.00.

Lot #227. Houbigant *Le Parfum d'Argeville* clear crystal bottle and stopper, 4.1' [10.4 cm], decorated with a shepherdess and sheep, near full, names in gold, bottom signed *Cristal Nancy.* Identical to Bacc. #219 [1913]. Est. $400.00-$500.00.

Lot #228. George Chevalier experimental bottle for Baccarat, 5.5" [14 cm], the front of the bottle showing two lovebirds in a nest of flowers, beautifully painted in white, grey, cream and gold, bottom signed *Baccarat* and *G. Chevalier*. Est. $2,000.00-$3,000.00.

Lot #229. Molinard *Habanita* huge clear glass bottle and stopper, 6.5" [16.5 cm], both the bottle and stopper designed as a cube with a raised square facet, empty, bottom signed *Crystal Nancy*. Est. $700.00-$900.00.

Lot #230. Guerlain *Liu* black glass bottle and stopper, 3.3" [8.3 cm], gold and black labels in excellent condition on front of bottle and top of stopper, Guerlain labels on bottom, empty, in its elegant black and gold presentation case of similar shape, unsigned. BACC #679 [1929]. Est. $500.00-$650.00.

Lot #231. Matchabelli *Empress of India* rare and fine quality amber glass bottle and stopper, 3.7" [9.4 cm], in the shape of a pyramid with four sides, Matchabelli crown and coat of arms molded on front, empty, bottom signed *Matchabelli* and *Made in France*. Est. $1,200.00-$1,500.00.

Lot #232. Houbigant *Subtilité* clear crystal bottle and stopper molded entirely as a sitting Buddha, 3.3" [8.5 cm], the stopper fitted with a brass ring, Baccarat emblem acid etched on bottom. Est. $400.00-$500.00.

Lot #233. Guerlain *Vague Souvenir* clear crystal bottle and 'Quadrilobe' stopper, 3.7" [9.4 cm], one of the important Guerlain fragrances, unopened, with label, in its brown flocked box with white satin interior, bottom signed *Baccarat* in emblem. Bacc. #24 [1908/1947]. Est. $300.00-$400.00.

Lot #234. Ybry *Devinez* ['Guess'] orange over white cased crystal bottle with inner stopper and metal overcap, 2.1" [11.2 cm] to top of stopper, metal overcap in orange enamel and inner stopper, empty, gold label, unsigned. Bacc. #583 [1925-1927]. Est. $1,200.00-$1,500.00.

Lot #235. Mori *Viens!* ['Come!'] clear glass bottle and clear and blue flower form stopper, 4.7" [12 cm], the flat bottle with two labels, signed *Baccarat* on the bottom and with paper label, in its original box. Est. $750.00-$1,000.00.

Lot #236. Christian Dior *Miss Dior* blue and clear crystal bottle and stopper of amphora shape, 7" [17.8 cm], empty, names in gold all in superb condition, bottom signed *Baccarat*. Bacc. #814 [1949]. Est. $800.00-$1,000.00.

Lot #237. Lournay *Fleur Vivant* ['Living Flower'] light green glass bottle and stopper overlaid in deep purple, 8.2" [20.1 cm], cork lined stopper, signed in cameo *Gallé*, empty, silver label on bottom, in a beautiful box the silk imprinted with *Lournay* and *Flacon de Gallé*. Extremely Rare. Est. $6,000.00-$8,000.00.

Lot #238. Peggy Hoyt *The Perfume of Aristocrats* clear crystal bottle and frosted crystal stopper, 4" [10 cm], the names on one side, and a whimsical design on the other marked *"Flowers,"* empty, Baccarat emblem on bottom. Bacc. #460 [1920]. Est. $500.00-$600.00.

Lot #239. D'Orsay *Toujours Fidèle* clear crystal pillow shaped bottle with sitting dog stopper, 3.5" [9 cm], stopper with brown patination, name and maker in enamel on front; Crystal Nancy emblem on botttom. Est. $400.00-$500.00.

COMMERCIAL PERFUME BOTTLES

Lot #240. Guerlain *Ambre* clear glass bottle and stopper, 3.7" [9.4 cm], the "square bottle," Guerlain tax stamps on the reverse, in its original box. Est. $150.00-$250.00.

Lot #241. Corday *Toujours Moi* clear glass bottle of flat round shape, 3.6" cm], with molded vegetal decoration on both bottle and stopper, brown pa gold label, empty, in its original brown box. Est. $300.00-$400.00.

Lot #242. Roger and Gallet unidentified fragrance clear glass bottle and crown shaped stopper, 8.7 [22 cm], the bottle in the shape of king holding an urn, bottom marked *Roger and Gallet France*. Est. $200.00-$300.00.

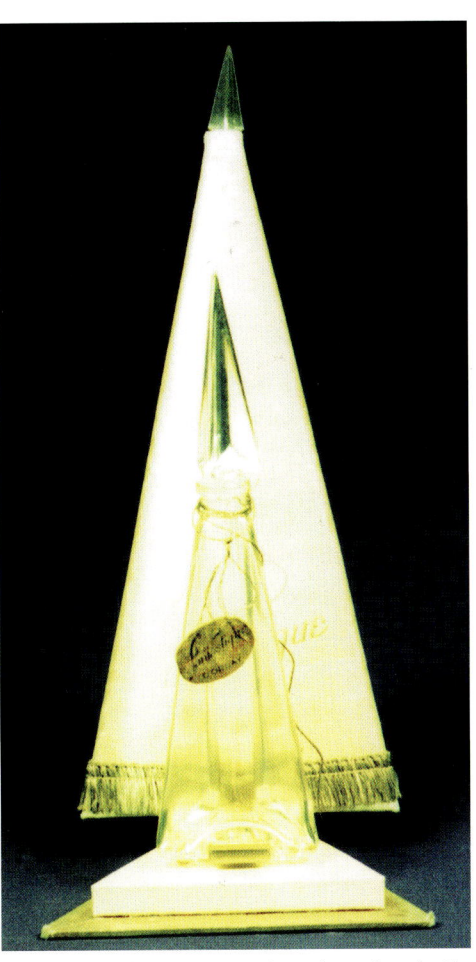

Lot #243. D'Orsay *Fantastique* clear glass bottle and stopper, 5.4" [13.7 cm], the bottle of elongated pyramid form with a sharply pointed stopper, empty, gold label, in its box, bottom signed *D'Orsay* in acid; circa 1952. Est. $400.00-$500.00.

Lot #244. *Severnyi* ['Northern'] Eau de Cologne glass bottle with white screw on stopper and overcap with a standing bear, 7.8" [19.8 cm], the bottle shaped like an iceberg, silver label on side, of Russian manufacture. Est. $200.00-$300.00.

Lot #245. Helena Rubenstein *Barynia* clear glass bottle and a cube stopper, 3.2" [8.1 cm], of hexagonal shape, name in gold enamel, in its elegant front opening box. Est. $200.00-$300.00.

Lot #246. Jean d'Albret *Casaque* clear and frosted glass bottle with frosted glass stopper in the shape of a crown, 4.3" [10.8 cm], full and sealed, gold label on front, bottom signed *d'Albret* in the mold, in its pink and black box covered with black netting. Est. $300.00-$375.00.

Lot #247. Renoir *Cattleya* clear glass bottle and stopper impressed with the coat of arms, full and sealed, label on front, in its front opening box. Est. $100.00-$200.00.

Lot #248. Houbigant *Demi Jour* peach glass perfume bottle and stopper, 4 [10.2 cm], label on front of bottle, empty, in its [tattered] original box. Es $200.00-$300.00.

Lot #249. Jean d'Albret *Ecusson* two piece set: eau de cologne, 4.4" [11.2 cm], and perfume, 3.5" [8.9 cm], both bottles molded with flying horses; tiny pamphlet included. Est. $75.00-$125.00.

Lot #250. Lee *Jasmine* with cork tipped stopper, in its box; Matchabelli *Po pourri*, label on bottom; Caron *Voeu de Noel*, opalescent glass bottle an stopper, bottom marked *Factice*, chip to the bottle lip. Est. $100.00-$200.00

Lot #251. Le Galion *Chypre* black glass bottle and stopper, 1.5" [3.8 cm], the stopper molded with a sailing ship and enameled in white, empty, label on front, bottom acid signed *Le Galion Paris.* Est. $100.00-$150.00.

Lot #252. D'Orsay *Intoxication* clear glass bottle and stopper of a pleated, star-like shape, 5" [12.7 cm], gold label hangs from a white cord at neck, full and sealed, in its original colorful box decorated with dancers, bottom signed *D'Orsay* in a circle. Est. $300.00-$400.00.

Lot #253. Schiaparelli *Shocking* clear glass bottle and stopper of rectangular form, 3" [7.6 cm], full and sealed, *S* label on front, in its charming box lined in pink satin shaped as a book decorated with hearts. Est. $200.00-$300.00.

Lot #254. Lazell's *Carnation Pink* clear glass bottle and stopper, 5.9" [15 cm], hexagonal shape with a faceted ball stopper, in its original box. Est. $150.00-$250.00.

Lot #255. Guerlain *Vol de Nuit* dark olive green glass bottle and stopper, 3.5" [8.9 cm], brass covered cap impressed *Guerlain*, the bottle molded with rays emanating from the center, brass medallion, unopened and full, in its zebra motif box. Est. $400.00-$500.00.

Lot #256. Lot of 18: *Byzance* by Byzance; Caron *Bellodgia* [no label]; Carven *Ma Griffe;* Couturier Perfumes *Shantung,* in its box; D'Orsay *Intoxication;* Guerlain *Chamade,* in its box, *Shalimar,* and a box for *L'Heure Bleu;* Ann Haviland *Perhaps;* Lanvin *Arpege,* in its box; *Lumiere du Jour,* in its red case; Mellier's *Sweet Crab Apple;* Myrurgia *Embrujo de Sevilla,* in its box; *Norell,* in is box; Paris *Eiffel Tower;* Patou *Moment Supreme;* De Rauch *Miss de Rauch,* two sizes. Eighteen items. Est. $200.00-$300.00.

Lot #257. Charbert *Amber* and *Fabulous,* in their boxes; Christian Dior *Diorissimo, Miss Dior* in box bottom; F. Millot *Crêpe de Chine,* in its box; unknown fragrance black glass bottle and stopper, in its box. Six items. Est. $300.00-$400.00.

Lot #258. Jovan *Sculptura* frosted glass atomizer, 6" [15.2 cm], shaped as a woman's torso, empty. Est. $100.00-$150.00.

Lot #259. Guerlain *Eau de Cologne Impériale* clear glass bottle and stopper, 6.2" [15.8 cm], apothecary shape, empty, intact antique label on front, bottom signed *Guerlain Paris France* in the mold; cf. Atlas and Monniot Guerlain, p. 60. Est. $300.00-$400.00.

Lot #260. Schiaparelli *Zut* ['Damn!!'] large size glass bottle and stopper in the shape of a woman's torso, 5.5" [14 cm], gold stopper, waist tied with green ribbon, empty, bottom signed *Schiaparelli Paris*. Est. $600.00-$750.00.

Lot #261. Guerlain *Le Mouchoir de Monsieur* ['A Gentleman's Handkerchief'] clear glass bottle and stopper, 5" [13 cm], of triangular shape, empty, label on bottom. This bottle, the *Escargot* or 'snail,' dates from 1902 by Pochet et du Courval; cf. Atlas & Monniot, p. 163. Est. $300.00-$400.00.

Lot #262. Luxor *Lybis* clear glass bottle and blue glass stopper, 5.4" [13.7 cm], the bottle impressed with violets on both sides and frosted, blue glass stopper, bottom marked *Made in Bohemia*. Cf. North, p. 193 for a 1924 ad. Est. $500.00-$750.00.

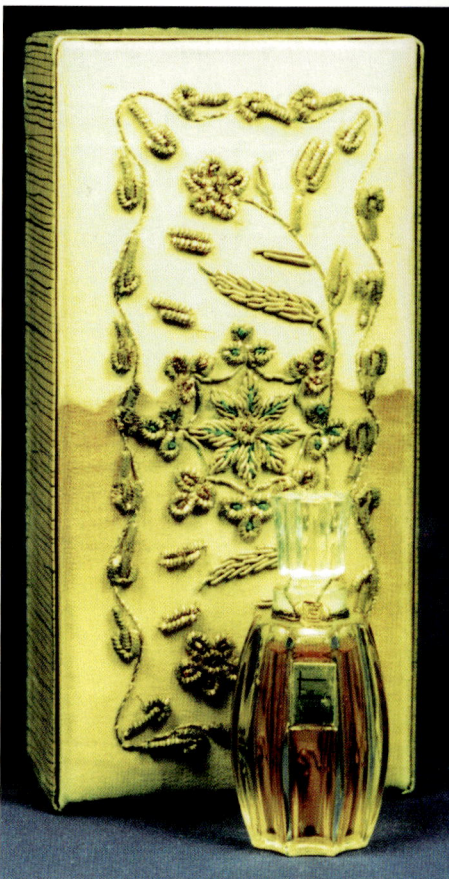

Lot #263. Houbigant *Le Parfum Idéal* clear glass bottle and stopper, 3.4" [8.6 cm], gold label at the center, in its box covered with flowers. Est. $100.00-$175.00.

Lot #264. Guerlain *Shalimar* clear and frosted glass bottle and stopper, 4.5" [11.4 cm], the bottle is the one typically used for *Ode* with its rosebud stopper, bottom signed *Guerlain,* in its box. Est. $125.00-$200.00.

Lot #265. Lucien Lelong *Tailspin* clear glass bottle and stopper, 2.8" [7.1 cm], Lelong logo molded into top of stopper, full and sealed, with label on front and on bottom, in its box [stained]. Est. $100.00-$200.00.

Lot #266. D'Orsay *Toujours Fidele* ['Always Faithful'] clear glass bottle and stopper, 2.5" [6.4 cm], in the famous octagonal shape, in its box. Est. $200.00-$300.00.

Lot #267. Corday *Zigane* clear glass bottle and ground glass stopper in the shape of a violin, 3" [7.6 cm], name in gold enamel, *Corday* written on the chin rest, empty, bottom signed *Corday* in the mold, in its deep pink box with pink satin lining. Est. $300.00-$400.00.

Lot #268. Mary Chess *Heliotrope* clear glass bottle and stopper, 2.9" [7.3 cm], in the shape of a chess rook, with perfume and sealed, label on front, bottom marked *Design Patent 129969,* in its box. Est. $150.00-$225.00.

Lot #269. Dralle Illusion *Rose* very small clear glass bottle and glass stopper, 2.6" [6.6 cm] in a bakelite lighthouse with gold label and red stone, tiny *Made in Germany* label. Est. $200.00-$300.00.

Lot #270. Seddy [Cairo] set of three Czechoslovakian glass perfume bottles with metal mounted applicators, each 2.7" [6.9 cm], the bottles molded with a swirled design and internally decorated with pink, yellow, and blue, metal mounts signed *Czechoslovakia,* case of purple velvet. Est. $600.00-$750.00.

Lot #271. Hermès *Calèche* clear glass bottle and stopper, extremely large and heavy, full and sealed, with label on front, in its very large box. Est. $150.00-$300.00.

Lot #272. Bienaimé *Chypre Impérial* clear glass bottle and stopper, 2.6" [6.7 cm], the bottle designed as three oval tiers with scalloped edges, similar stopper, some perfume, with its label, in its drop-front gold foil box decorated with oriental motifs. Est. $100.00-$200.00.

Lot #273. Revillon *Carnet de Bal* ['Dance Card'] clear glass bottle and stopper, 2.4" [4.8 cm], the bottle and stopper shaped as a brandy snifter inverted, full, in its yellow box [interior stain]. Est. $100.00-$200.00.

Lot #274. Jacques Griffe *Grilou* clear glass bottle and stopper, 2.5" [6.4 cm], of square shape, with perfume, names in enamel on front, in its red box lined in gray satin. Est. $100.00-$200.00.

Lot #275. *Niki de St. Phalle* eau de toilette blue glass bottle with gold stopper, 2.9" [7.4 cm], the front enameled with two very colorful snakes entwined, in its original box. Est. $200.00-$300.00.

Lot #276. Fabergé *Woodhue* bath perfume clear glass bottle and metal stopper, 5.8" [14.7 cm], a classical ewer shape, names in gold, bottom signed *Fabergé,* in its box. Est. $75.00-$150.00.

Lot #277. Gourielli *Something Blue* clear glass bottle and stopper, 3.3" [8.3 cm], the bottle molded with a heart-shaped medallion showing a smiling cupid, empty, label on bottom. Est. $250.00-$350.00.

Lot #278. Unidentified maker *Lilas* ['Lilac'] milk glass bottle in the shape of an elephant, 7" [17.8 cm], tiny label on back, empty. Incredibly, this is still in perfect shape. Est. $250.00-$500.00.

Lot #279. Jacques Fath *Canasta* clear glass bottle and stopper, 4.2" [10.6 cm], designed with pleats all around, gold label, in its original box. Est. $150.00-$250.00.

Lot #280. Lancôme *Magie* clear crystal bottle, inner stopper, and overcap, of a gently twisted standing rectangle shape, 4.5" [11.5 cm], with its gold label on top, in its sumptuous box of pink silk interior, exterior with painted starburst and sequins. Est. $400.00-$600.00.

Lot #281. Guerlain *Fleur de Feu* ['Flower of Fire'] clear glass bottle and stopper, 4.5" [11.4 cm], full and sealed, label around neck, bottom signed *Guerlain,* in its gray box lined in white silk. Circa 1948. Est. $350.00-$450.00.

Lot #282. Vigny *Le Golliwogg* frosted glass bottle and black glass stopper, 2.9" to top of hair [7.4 cm], molded as a Golliwogg, empty, crisp label on front. Est. $300.00-$400.00.

Lot #283. Palmer *May Bloom* clear glass bottle and stopper, the bottle molded *Palmer* on the reverse and with tax stamp for March 1, 1899, in its box. Est. $150.00-$250.00.

Lot #284. Prince Matchabelli *Stradivari* clear and frosted glass bottle and stopper, 3.9" [10 cm], a large 4 oz. size in the famous crown shape, bottom signed *Matchabelli.* Est. $200.00-$300.00.

Lot #285. Jeanne Lanvin *Arpège* clear glass bottle and stopper encased in gold, 2.2" [5.6 cm], near full, in its tiny box. Est. $800.00-$1,000.00.

Lot #286. Leon Laraine *Triomphe* clear and frosted crystal bottle and red crystal stopper in the form of the Arc de Triomphe, 4.5" [11.4 cm], , of Czechoslovakian manufacture but unsigned. Est. $125.00-$225.00.

Lot #287. Caron *Fête des Roses* ['Celebration of Roses'] clear glass bottle and stopper, 4.1" [10.4 cm], entirely enameled in brilliant gold, empty, label on bottom. Est. $250.00-$350.00.

Lot #288. Elizabeth Arden *Blue Grass* clear glass bottle, glass inner stopper, and turquoise glass overcap, 3.3" [8.4 cm], label on front, with some perfume, bottom marked *Made in France*. Est. $100.00-$200.00.

Lot #289. Lander *Jasmin* frosted glass bottle and stopper in the shape of a pensive woman, 4" [10.2 cm], the stopper has a cork tip, label on bottom. Est. $100.00-$200.00.

Lot #290. Lorenzy-Palanca *Soyons Discrets* ['Let's Be Discrete"] clear glass bottle and stopper, 8.5" [21.6 cm], of decanter form and possibly factice, gigantic label on front. Est. $200.00-$300.00.

Lot #291. Schiaparelli *Si* ['If'] clear glass bottle and original atomizer, 5.5" [14 cm], shaped as a Chianti bottle, empty, bottom molded *Schiaparelli*. Est. $400.00-$600.00.

Lot #292. Bourjois *Evening in Paris* talcum, Carven *Ma Griffe*, Chanel *No. 22*, Mary Dunhill *Frou Frou de Gardenia*, Guerlain *Vol de Nuit*, Richard Hudnut *Gemey* [chips under stopper], Lanvin *Arpege*, two different sizes, Lucien Lelong *Indiscret* cologne, Marcel Rochas *Femme*, in its box. 10 items. Est. $150.00-$250.00.

Lot #293. Nanette [London] *Devon Violets* yellow glass bottle impressed with tulips and its reddish plastic stopper, 2.3" [5.8 cm], pretty label on front, bottle impressed with tulips. Est. $125.00-200.00.

Lot #294. Bourjois *Evening in Paris* gift set in the form of a sailor's hat, 11" diameter [28 cm], including talcum, Eau de Cologne, powder [opened], perfume, lipstick [used], and purse perfume, in their box. This is one of the harder to find *Evening in Paris* sets. Est. $800.00-$1,000.00.

Lot #295. Lubin *Ouvrez-Moi* ['Open me'] black glass perfume bottle disguised as a purse, 3.5" [8.9 cm], the bottom molded *Lubin;* this perfume is circa 1937. Est. $1,000.00-$1,500.00.

Lot #296. Tilford *High Heels* clear glass bottle with gold cap, 2.4" [6.1 cm], "the only American fragrance featured at the Brussels World's Fair," unopened, in its box and outer box. Est. $200.00-$300.00.

Lot #297. Vigny *Le Golliwogg* frosted glass bottle and black glass stopper, 5" to top of hair [7.6 cm], molded as a Golliwogg, empty, crisp label on front, bottom signed *Vigny,* in its mint condition box. Est. $1,250.00-$1,750.00.

Lot #298. Langlois *Rose* frosted glass bottle and stopper, 3.1" [8 cm], the oval bottle designed with a clear diamond-shaped window, stopper with a molded flower, empty, beautiful gold label, in its brown and cream silk box. Est. $300.00-$400.00.

Lot #299. House of Tre-Jur, frosted glass bottle and stopper in the form of a woman, 2.5" [6.3 cm]; delicate long dauber intact; empty, signed *Made in France* in acid etched on bottom. Est. $250.00-$350.00.

Lot #300. Parfumerie Dr. Josef Sutter *Eau de Cologne Russe* rare clear glass bottle and stopper, 4.5" [11.4 cm], with a red and gold label, the stopper molded as a woman removing her hat, fine quality molding, empty. Est. $500.00-$650.00.

Lot #301. Eroy *Adorée* clear glass bottle and frosted glass stopper, 4.2" [10.7 cm], the stopper as a kneeling nude woman; this figure is often thought of as Isadora Duncan. Est. $200.00-$250.00.

Lot #302. Houbigant *Parfum Présence* clear glass bottle and stopper, 3.5" [8.9 cm], empty, in its green moiré box with rope ties; circa 1930's. With a business card from A. Noel Shaw "With all good wishes for Xmas 1937." Est. $100.00-$200.00.

Lot #303. Watkins *Belle de Nuit* ['Beautiful Woman of the Night'] clear glass bottle and black glass stopper, 6.3" [16 cm], pretty label on front, in its orange box with black and gold flowers and an advertising pamphlet. Est. $150.00-$250.00.

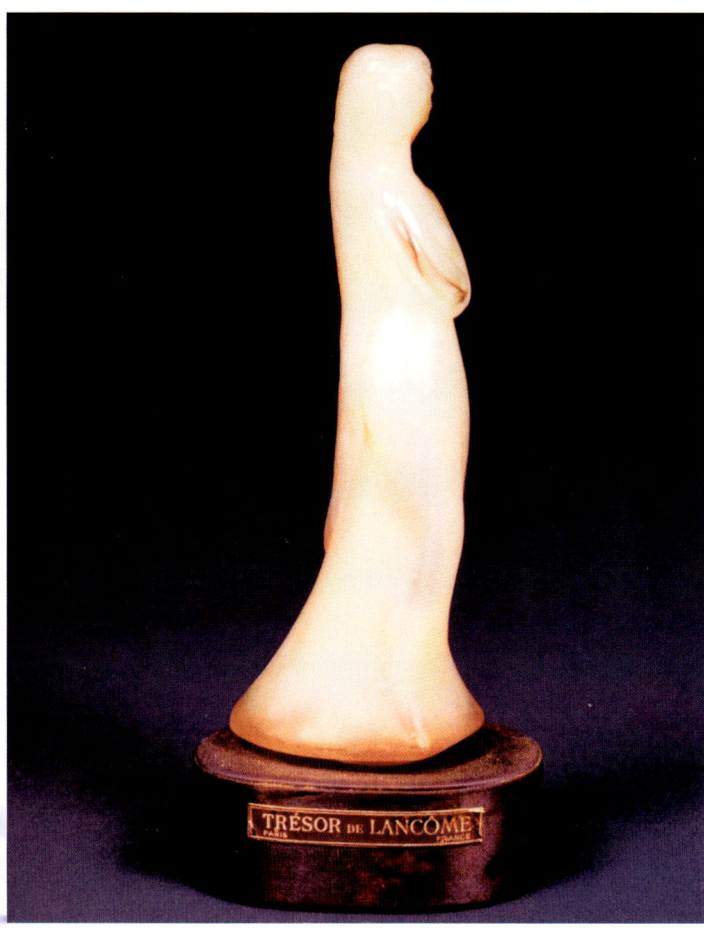

Lot #304. Lancôme *Trésor* milky opalescent glass bottle and stopper in the form of a maiden with very long hair, 6.7" total height [17 cm], empty, label on the pedestal which is also the bottle's stopper. Est. $1,000.00-$1,500.00.

Lot #305. Lilly Daché *Dashing* beautiful composition over glass bottle, 7" [17.8 cm], the dog sitting up and holding a letter addressed to Lilly Daché, the dog made out of composition. Est. $3,000.00-$4,000.00.

Lot #306. Hattie Carnegie *Hypnotic* clear glass bottle and stopper, 4.2" [10.7 cm], in the shape of a woman's head and shoulders, entirely covered in gold enamel, empty, the name molded in raised letters around the bottom of the bottle, in its seldom seen light blue box [stain on inside of box bottom] with label on bottom. Est. $800.00-$1,000.00.

Lot #307. Lucien Lelong *Jabot* frosted glass bottle and stopper with overcap, 2.3" [5.8 cm], the entire bottle in the shape of an elaborate bow, inner stopper with long dauber, decal label on front and on bottom, empty; this one-half ounce size is not often seen, especially in its original oval box. Est. $800.00-$1,000.00.

Lot #308. Schiaparelli *Shocking* glass bottle in the form of a dress dummy, with gold cap, 3.5" [8.9 cm], with its tape measure label and in its glass dome, in its mint condition box and box cover. Est. $400.00-$500.00.

Lot #309. Gilbert Orcel *Coup de Chapeau* white glass bottle, inner stopper and overcap, 5" [12.5 cm], molded as the bust of a woman, highlights enameled in gold, empty, bottom molded *Orcel Made in France*. Est. $400.00-$500.00.

Lot #310. Marquay ['Le Couturier du Parfum'] *Prince Douka* very large size clear glass bottle and frosted glass stopper, 6.4" [16.3 cm], designed in the shape of a swami, cream satin cape decorated with rhinestones; full and sealed, bottom marked *factice*, in its box. Est. $600.00-$800.00.

Lot #311. Matchabelli *Dutchess of York* orange glass bottle with gold stopper, 3.7" [9.4 cm], two labels on front, bottom marked *Prince Matchabelli Made in France*, in its original blue box. Est. $500.00-$600.00.

Lot #313. Worth *Dans la Nuit* clear glass bottle and stopper, 4.3" [10.9 cm], the bottle molded with stars, plastic-tipped stopper impressed with a *W.* Est. $200.00-$300.00.

Lot #312. Marcel Guerlain *Le Roi le Veult* ['The King Wishes it'] clear glass bottle and stopper, 3" [7.6 cm], in the shape of a crown, empty, label on bottom, in its original box. Est. $3,500.00-$4,500.00.

Lot #315. Clamy *Femmes Aillées* ['Wingèd Ladies'] frosted and clear glass bottle and stopper, 2.5" [6.4 cm], the original produced in 1913 by L. Gaillard; this example was produced in 1986 by the Verreries Brosse. Est. $75.00-$150.00.

Lot #314. Nina Ricci *Eau de Coeur Joie* clear glass bottle and ball stopper, 6.5" [16.5 cm], beautiful label at center, bottom signed *Lalique.* Est. $200.00-$300.00.

Lot #316. Nina Ricci *L'Air du Temps* ['The Air of Time'] frosted glass bottle and metal cap, 1.9" [4.8 cm], the bottle designed in a sunburst motif; this is a very early example, and a very rare size, of this perfume. Utt #NR-110. Est. $200.00-$300.00.

Lot #317. Nina Ricci *Farouche* clear glass bottle and stopper, 2.6" [6.6 cm], of urn shape with an octagonal stopper, full and sealed, name in gold enamel on front, bottom signed *Lalique* in the mold, in its red flocked box. Est. $150.00-$250.00.

Lot #318. Coty *L'Origan* clear glass bottle and frosted glass stopper, 3.4" [8.6 cm], the stopper molded with two butterflies, with its label and in its black leather case. Est. $150.00-$250.00.

Lot #319. Worth *Je Reviens* ['I Will Come Back'] smoky blue glass bottle and opaque turquoise stopper, 3.7" [9.4 cm], this flat round form synonymous with Worth perfumes, *Worth* in molded block letters on front, full and sealed, bottom molded *R. Lalique*, in its turquoise box lined with white satin. Utt #W-2. Est. $250.00-$350.00.

Lot #320. Cristal Lalique *Deux Fleurs* clear and frosted perfume bottle and stopper, 3.5" [8.9 cm], formed of two overlapping flowers with the stopper identical to the flowers' center, originally designed by René Lalique in 1935, bottom engraved *Lalique*. Utt # CL-108. Est. $100.00-$200.00.

Lot #321. Worth *Sans Adieu* brilliant emerald green glass bottle and stopper of columnar shape, 5.4" [13.7 cm], the stopper molded as a series of seven rings [the last one is the lip of the bottle], the largest size of this model, near full and sealed with black ribbon under the label, signed *R. Lalique* in the mold, in its seldom seen green wood box and chrome plinth. Utt #W-8. Est. $3,000.00-$4,000.00.

Lot #322. Nina Ricci *Coeur Joie* the two-hearted bottle with its gold cap, 2.2" [5.6 cm], in its plastic case marked *Nina Ricci.* This is the size that is missing from most collections. Est. $200.00-$300.00.

Lot #323. Worth *Imprudence* clear glass bottle and stopper in a design of concentric rings which are enameled in silver, 2.8" [7 cm], stopper with the original of two designs for this bottle, empty, molded signature *R. Lalique,* in its blue and gold box. Est. $800.00-$1,200.00.

Lot #324. Worth *Requête* ['Request'] clear glass bottle and stopper, 2.9" [7.4 cm], scallops enameled in blue, full and sealed with original double tag labels, bottom signed *Lalique* in the mold; in its box. Utt #W-105. Est. $1,000.00-$1,250.00.

Lot #325. Forvil *Mimosa* clear and frosted glass cylindrical bottle and stopper, 4" [10.3 cm], decorated with stylized daisies, brown patination, empty, molded *R. Lalique.* Utt #F-5. Est. $800.00-$1,000.00.

Lot #326. Worth *Dans La Nuit* ['In the Night'] blue enameled glass bottle and stopper, 3" [7.6 cm], a crescent moon and the perfume name molded on the stopper. Est. $400.00-$600.00.

Lot #327. Maison Lalique *Glycines* 'Wisteria' frosted glass bottle and stopper, 4.7" [12 cm], molded with wisteria vines, apparently unsigned. Est. $1,500.00-$2,000.00.

Lot #328. Houbigant *La Belle Saison* ['The Beautiful Season'] clear and frosted glass bottle and stopper of indented rectangular form, 3.9" [10 cm], the portrait of a young woman with flowers at center and with rays of leaves and flowers emanating outward, empty, superb gold label on reverse, in its beautiful green windowed box, signed in the mold *R. Lalique;* circa 1926. Utt #H-1. Est. $4,000.00-$6,000.00.

Lot #329. Maison Lalique *Palerme* clear glass bottle and stopper, 4.6" [11.7 cm], the teardrop shaped bottle molded with strands of pearls in three rows, stopper also similarly molded, bottom molded *R. Lalique.* Utt #ML-518. Est. $700.00-$850.00.

Lot #330. Molinard *Le Provençale* frosted glass atomizer designed as an oval frieze of nude maidens, 5.3" [13.5 cm], bottom acid-signed *Molinard Lalique France.* Est. $500.00-$750.00.

Lot #331. Renaud *Sur 2 Notes* ['On 2 Notes'] clear and frosted oval glass bottle with a spire stopper, 5.4" [13.7 cm], molded with leaves, label on front, some perfume, signed *Lalique;* circa 1940's. Utt #Rel-1. Est. $1,000.00-$1,500.00.

Lot #332. Delettrez *Inalda* rare clear glass bottle and stopper, 3.6" [9.1 cm], the shape of the bottle formed by indented rows and decorated with dots in black enamel, cone shaped stopper also decorated with enamel dots, empty, bottom molded *R. Lalique.* Utt #DEL-1. Est. $1,750.00-$2,250.00.

Lot #333. Maison Lalique *Marquita* frosted glass bottle and stopper, 3.4" [8.5 cm], a design with overlapping leaves, bottle signed *R. Lalique* in the mold and in script on the bottom. Est. $1,000.00-$1,250.00.

Lot #334. D'Orsay *Les Fleurs* clear and frosted glass tester bar for five fragrances, 8.8" x 2" x 1.8" [22.3 x 5.1 x 4.5 cm], entirely molded with a design of thorny branches, with the word *D'Orsay* spelled out as a part of the design on one side, the stoppers shaped as flowers and each stopper with a dauber and with the name of each fragrance molded in the center of the flower, numbered *1 Chypre; 2 Fleurs de France; 3 Les Fleurs; 4 Le Chevalier; 5 Le Lys,* all with daubers, signed *Lalique* in the mold at the top. Utt Fig. 112. Est. $2,500.00-$3,000.00.

Lot #335. Roger and Gallet *Le Jade* green glass perfume bottle and stopper, 3.2" [8.2 cm], molded as a snuff bottle with a giant peacock on one side, the bottom signed *R. L. Paris.* Est. $4,000.00-$5,000.00.

Lot #336. *Molinard* de Molinard clear and frosted glass bottle and stopper, 4.4" [11.2 cm], molded with a pattern of nudes all around, bottom signed *Creation Lalique,* full and sealed, in its original box. Est. $400.00-$500.00.

Lot #337. Guerlain *Le Bouquet de Faunes* frosted glass bottle and stopper, 3.9" [9.9 cm], the bottle with four heads of women and satyrs. Est. $750.00-$950.00.

Lot #338. Maison Lalique frosted glass atomizer, 4" [10.2 cm], two small sparrows on either side, atomizer marked *Made in France,* signed near the base *R. Lalique France.* Not seen in the 1932 catalogue or in the Utt book. Est. $800.00-$1,200.00.

Lot #339. Jay Thorpe & Co. *Jaytho* clear and frosted glass bottle and stopper, 4" [10.2 cm], the entire bottle molded as a bouquet of tulips and the stopper as a bud, rich amber patina, *JATHO* molded vertically in front, bottom molded *R. Lalique.* Utt #JT-1. Est. $1,000.00-$1,200.00.

Lot #340. Maison Lalique *Camille* rare dark blue glass bottle and stopper, 2.2" [5.5 cm], the highly sculptured design resembling that of a shell, etched signature *R. Lalique.* Utt #ML 516. Est. $4,000.00-$5,000.00.

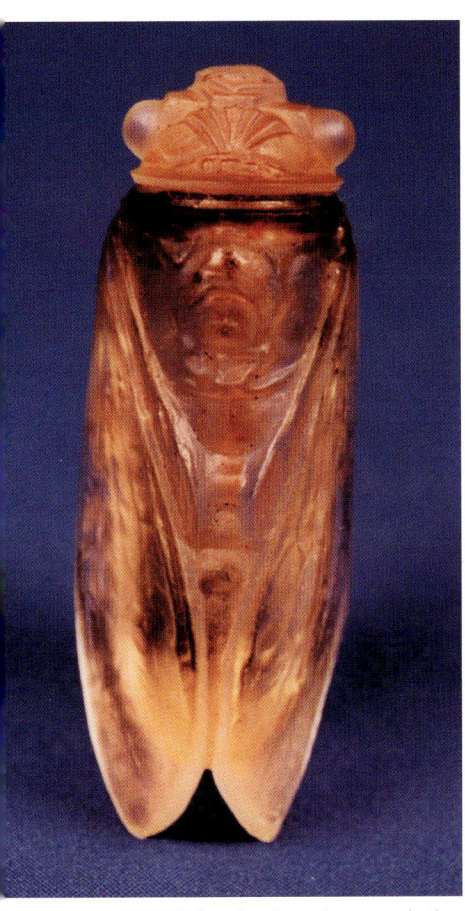

Lot #341. Frosted glass bottle and stopper in the shape of a locust, 2.5" [6.4 cm], beautifully molded, *Deposé* and the initials *MP* molded on the reverse side under the wings. Est. $2,500.00-$3,000.00.

Lot #342. D'Orsay *Ambre d'Orsay* black glass bottle and stopper, 5.2" [13.2 cm], with classical maidens molded into four corners, stopper with flowers, bottom edge molded *Lalique* and opposite edge molded *Ambre d'Orsay*, empty. Est. $2,000.00-$3,000.00.

Lot #343. Woodworth *Tous Les Bouquets* ['All Flowers'] clear and frosted glass bottle and stopper, 5" [12.7 cm], with a frieze of young children, with gray patina, signed in the mold *J. Viard*. Est. $1,750.00-$2,250.00.

Lot #344. Benoit *Nuit de Paques* ['Easter Evening'] black glass bottle and stopper, 4.4" [11.2 cm], extremely rare bottle of flask form, the back molded *H. Benoit Paris*. According to C. Lefkowith, this is circa 1925 and only about five exist of this model. Est. $3,500.00-$4,500.00.

Lot #345. Lydes *Ambre des Pagodes* clear glass bottle and stopper, 2.7" [6.9 cm], the bottle of a round pillow form decorated with bands of ridges, the stopper a nude maiden with flowing hair, near full, label on bottom, by Constant Dépinoix, unsigned. Est. $1,500.00-$2,000.00.

Lot #346. Lengyel *Parfum Impérial* clear and frosted glass bottle and stopper, 3.4" [8.6 cm], molded with the Russian Imperial double eagle on both sides, the stopper shaped as a Russian crown, empty, full and sealed, with its label, bottom signed *R. Lalique* in the mold, in its exquisite gold foil box. Complete, rare, and mint. Utt #Len-1. Est. $3,000.00-$4,000.00.

Lot #347. Jean de Paris *Sous le Gui* ['Under the Mistletoe'] black glass bottle and inner stopper and overcap, 4.1" [10.4 cm], the stopper molded with mistletoe and enameled in gold, names in gold enamel on the outside of the bottle, with red tassel, unsigned. Est. $5,000.00-$7,500.00.

Lot #348. Robj *Le Secret de Robj* clear glass bottle and stopper, 3.6" [9.1 cm], beautiful label at center, in its book-form box with outer cover [small paper fragment missing]; inside there is a quote by Albert Samain and this: *Toute chose sur terre possède son attrait, La vie a son mystere et Robj a son "secret."* ['Every thing on earth has its charm, Life has its mystery and Robj has its secret.']. Est. $2,000.00-$3,000.00.

Lot #349. Isabey *Jasmin* clear and frosted glass bottle and stopper, 6.5" [16.5 cm], the faceted bottle with twelve panels, a frosted band of leaves with patina on the bottle and on the stopper, half full of perfume, label on bottom, in its very rare and stained Art Deco box. Never before seen; undocumented in the literature. Est. $6,000.00-$7,500.00.

Lot #350. Harriet Hubbard Ayer *Coeur d'Or* ['Heart of Gold'] clear and frosted glass bottle and stopper, 3.4" [8.7 cm], with grey stain, *HHA* monogram and with a *Made in France* paper label. Est. $800.00-$1,200.00.

Lot #351. Fragonard *Orchidée* black glass bottle and stopper, 3" [7.6 cm], stopper molded with fruit laden branches and covered in gold enamel, pretty gold label, empty, in its box [edges torn]. Est. $400.00-$600.00.

Lot #352. Dubarry *Golden Morn Perfume* clear glass bottle and frosted figural stopper, 4.5" [11.4 cm], the stopper is a figural Pierrot, gold labels front and bottom, in its original box. Est. $6,000.00-$8,000.00.

Lot #353. Claire *Orée* ['The Skirt'] clear and frosted glass bottle and stopper, 3.2" [8.2 cm], molded with a lady in flowing dress differently on both sides, the back with three United States proprietary stamps [series 1914], empty, stopper signed *Lalique,* in its box. Est. $4,000.00-$5,000.00.

Lot #354. Odéon *Pour Amour* ['For Love'] frosted glass bottle and stopper, 3.6" [9.1 cm], the bottle molded with pine branches and pine cones, the stopper designed as a single pine cone, empty, rich grayish green patina, label on bottom, possibly by J. Viard. Est. $2,000.00-$3,000.00.

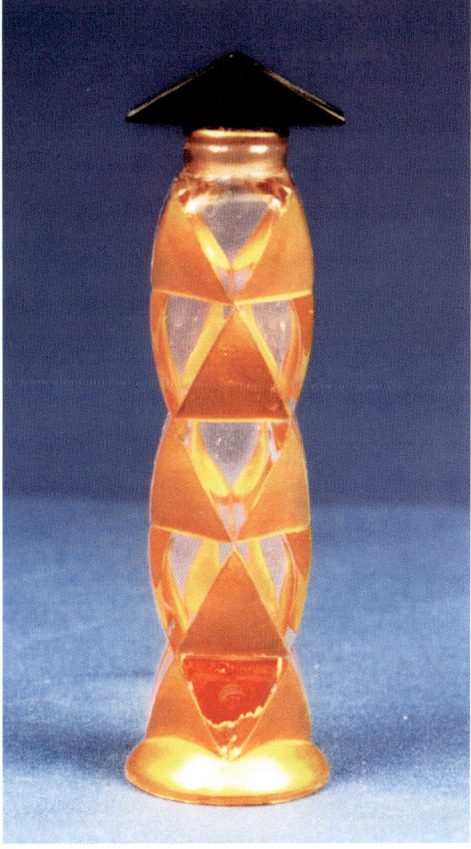

Lot #355. Rimmel *Naniva* extremely rare perfume bottle and stopper, 3.4" [8.6 cm], shaped as an elegant urn in yellow glass and with brown patina, beautiful oval label, bottom unmarked. Est. $1,500.00-$2,000.00.

Lot #356. Les Parfums de Rosine *Arlequinade* clear glass bottle and black glass stopper, 5.8" [14.7 cm], alternate panels enameled in gold, empty, partial label at bottom. Est. $3,000.00-$4,000.00.

Lot #357. De Seghers *Pinx* clear and frosted glass bottle, 3.9" [10 cm], molded with abstract geometric motifs in the cubist style, labels front and back [worn and faint], bottom signed *A. Jollivet* in acid. Est. $1,000.00-$1,250.00.

Lot #358. Serez *Notre Dame* ['Our Lady'] very fine quality blue glass bottle, inner stopper, and overcap, 4.7" [12 cm], a very unusual design in which the bottle and cap are covered in a lace-like effect, [stopper with a bruise], bottom marked *Made in France*. This company appears to be unlisted in the existing literature. Est. $3,000.00-$5,000.00.

CZECHOSLOVAKIAN PERFUME BOTTLES

Lot #359. Clear glass bottle and metal stopper with two yellow glass beads dangling from chains, 2.5" [6.4 cm], bottom marked *IRice* in the mold, neck signed *Czechoslovakia*. Est. $100.00-$200.00.

Lot #360. The New York World's Fair of 1939 souvenir perfume bottle, 2.6" [6.6 cm], bottom of bottle marked *IRice* in the mold, emblazoned with the monogram of the fair. Est. $100.00-$150.00.

Lot #361. Clear glass bottle encased in a metal framework and metal stopper with its long dauber, 3" [7.6 cm], the front of the bottle impressed with three blue stones, bottom marked *Patent Pending* in the mold. Est. $100.00-$150.00.

Lot #362. Miniature Czechoslovakian bottle, 3" [15.2 cm], decorated with a yellow stone and two beaded dancers, signed *Czechoslovakia* on a tag at the cap. Est. $175.00-$250.00.

Lot #363. Miniature bottle and stopper with its dauber, 2.5" [6.4 cm], decorated with blue stones and beads, bottom marked *IRice*. Est. $150.00-$225.00.

Lot #364. Miniature glass bottle and stopper, 1.8" [4.6 cm], encased in metal and decorated with carved stones and pearls, unsigned. Est. $250.00-$350.00.

Lot #365. Miniature clear glass bottle and screw on stopper encased in a metal framework, 2.2" [5.6 cm], impressed with yellow, red, and black stones, neck signed *Czechoslovakia*. Est. $125.00-$225.00.

Lot #366. Clear glass bottle and metal stopper, 4.4" [11.2 cm], the bottle in a metal framework and decorated with glass beads, featuring a picture of a lady with billowing hair, bottom signed *Irving Rice Co.* Est. $100.00-$200.00.

Lot #367. Pair of clear glass bottles and stoppers, 5.3" [13.5 cm], of square shape with imposing stoppers, bottoms of both with IRice label. Two Items. Est. $100.00-$200.00.

Lot #368. Clear glass bottle and metal stopper, 2.1" [5.3 cm], the front with an impressed lapis glass medallion and lapis beads, neck signed *Czechoslovakia.* Est. $150.00-$250.00.

Lot #369. Square clear glass bottle and stopper, 2.1" [5.3 cm], the front decorated with purple and clear rhinestones, stopper also with purple stone, neck marked *Austria* and with paper label also. Est. $150.00-$250.00.

Lot #370. Clear glass bottle and metal stopper impressed with a blue jewel, 2.3" [5.8 cm], the front of the bottle with flowers and a cameo like image of a woman, neck impressed *Czechoslovakia.* Est. $150.00-$250.00.

Lot #371. Miniature crystal bottle and red crystal stopper, 2.4" [6 cm], the red heart-shaped stopper with its dauber, bottom with silver *Aristo* label and signed *Czechoslovakia* in an oval. Est. $175.00-$250.00.

Lot #372. Clear crystal bottle and pink crystal stopper, 4.4" [11.2 cm], both the bottle and heart-shaped stopper impressed with roses, dauber lacking, bottom signed *Czechoslovakia*. Est. $200.00-$300.00.

Lot #373. Pair of clear crystal bottles with diamond shaped peach stoppers, each 3.5" [16.5 cm], daubers lacking, both with *Morlee* label. Two items. Est. $150.00-$250.00.

Lot #374. Miniature yellow crystal perfume bottle and stopper, 2.1" [5.3 cm], cut with a star motif, apparently unsigned. Est. $100.00-$200.00.

Lot #375. Small pink crystal bottle and stopper, 4" [10.2 cm], the base highly cut, bottom with *Sico* label and signed *Czechoslovakia* in a circle. Est. $125.00-$200.00.

Lot #376. Small violet crystal perfume bottle and stopper, 3.5" [8.9 cm], the stopper with its dauber, bottom unsigned. Est. $125.00-$200.00.

Lot #377. Pair of clear crystal bottles and stoppers, 5" [12.7 cm], the stoppers with a flower design, bottoms with stickers saying *US Zone Germany*. Two items. Est. $125.00-$200.00.

Lot #378. Clear crystal bottle and blue crystal stopper, 4.5" [11.4 cm], dauber lacking, bottom signed *Czechoslovakia* and with IRice paper label; clear crystal bottle and green crystal stopper, 3.8" [9.6 cm], dauber lacking, signed *Czechoslovakia*. Two items. Est. $100.00-$200.00.

Lot #379. Peach crystal bottle and stopper, 7" [17.8 cm], of simple geometric form, dauber lacking, bottom unsigned. Est. $100.00-$200.00.

Lot #380. Peach glass bottle and stopper, 5.2" [13.2 cm], the base cut with a star motif [chip to bottle], with its dauber, apparently unsigned. Est. $100.00-$200.00.

Lot #381. Clear crystal bottle and black crystal stopper, 5.2" [13.2 cm], the base with a simple design of lines, bottom signed *Czechoslovakia* in a circle. Est. $150.00-$250.00.

Lot #382. Pair of pink crystal bottles and stoppers, 6.4" [16.3 cm], both bottle and stopper highly cut, one with dauber, bottoms of both bottles signed *Czechoslovakia*. Two items. Est. $300.00-$400.00.

Lot #383. Clear crystal bottle and black crystal stopper, 4" [10.2 cm], dauber lacking, both bottle and stopper cut with a spiral design, bottom signed *Czecho-slovakia*. Est. $100.00-$200.00.

Lot #384. Pair of peach glass bottles and stoppers, both bottle and stopper of fan shape, daubers lacking, both adorned with a red corral glass medallion shaped as flowers, apparently unsigned. Two items. Est. $500.00-$600.00.

Lot #385. Pretty charcoal grey bottle and stopper, 4.4" [11.2 cm], the bottle impressed with squares, the stopper molded with flowers, with its dauber, bottom signed *Czechoslovakia* in an oval. Est. $250.00-$350.00.

Lot #386. Clear crystal bottle and peach crystal stopper, 4.2" [10.7 cm], the stopper of cube form, apparently unsigned. Est. $100.00-$200.00.

Lot #387. Clear crystal bottle and stopper, 5.5" [14 cm], the stopper intaglio cut with roses, with its dauber, bottom signed *Czechoslovakia* in a circle. Est. $250.00-$350.00.

Lot #388. Clear crystal bottle and stopper, 5.4" [13.7 cm], the tall stopper impressed with a floral design, dauber lacking, bottom signed *Czechoslovakia*. Est. $100.00-$200.00.

Lot #389. Clear crystal bottle and yellow crystal stopper, 6" [15.2 cm], the stopper with a cut out portion, apparently unsigned. Est. $300.00-$400.00.

Lot #390. Large clear crystal bottle and stopper, 7.2" [18.3 cm], the stopper with an open loop of cut glass, with its dauber, bottom signed *Czechoslovakia* in a circle. Est. $300.00-$450.00.

Lot #391. Clear and frosted crystal bottle and stopper, 5.3" [13.5 cm], the stopper in the shape of a wreath of leaves, with its dauber, bottom with *Silverleaf* label and signed *Czechoslovakia*. Est. $200.00-$300.00.

Lot #392. Light yellow bottle and stopper, 5.5" [14 cm], the stopper decorated with intaglio cut violets, the bottle with three feet, with its dauber, apparently unsigned. Est. $175.00-$250.00.

Lot #393. Clear crystal bottle and stopper, 5.4" [13.7 cm], the stopper highly cut in rows, with its dauber, bottom signed *Czechoslovakia* in an oval. Est. $150.00-$250.00.

Lot #394. Blue crystal bottle and stopper, 5" [12.7 cm], the identical star pattern cut into stopper and bottle, dauber lacking, signed *Czechoslovakia* in a circle. Est. $200.00-$300.00.

Lot #395. Blue crystal bottle and stopper, 6" [15.2 cm], the stopper molded with a flower, dauber lacking, signed *Czechoslovakia* in an oval. Est. $300.00-$400.00.

Lot #396. Blue crystal bottle and clear crystal stopper, 5.6" [14.2 cm], the stopper intaglio cut with a nude, dauber lacking, bottom signed *Czechoslovakia* in an oval. Est. $200.00-$300.00.

Lot #397. Ingrid blue crystal atomizer bottle, 5" [12.7 cm], molded all over with roses and cut with four smooth sides, with *Ingrid* label on one side. Est. $350.00-$450.00.

Lot #398. Clear glass bottle and fire red glass stopper, 4" [10.2 cm], the bottle cut with simple facets, the stopper shaped as leaves, dauber lacking, unsigned. Est. $250.00-$350.00.

Lot #399. Clear crystal bottle and unusual teal green stopper, 4.1" [10.4 cm], bottle and stopper fancifully cut, bottom signed *Czechoslovakia* in a circle. Est. $200.00-$300.00.

Lot #400. Three piece set of Czechoslovakian glass: covered powder dish, 3.4" [8.6 cm] and two perfume bottles, 6" [15.2 cm], all of green frosted glass, molded with flowers all around, bottoms molded *IRice* and *Czechoslovakia*. Three items. Est. $200.00-$300.00.

Lot #401. Clear crystal bottle and stopper, 4.8" [12.2 cm], the stopper intaglio cut with a dancer and flowers, bottom signed *Czechoslovakia* in an oval. Est. $200.00-$300.00.

Lot #402. Green crystal bottle and stopper, 6.2" [15.7 cm], the stopper shaped as a leaf, dauber lacking, bottom signed *Czechoslovakia* in a circle. Est. $150.00-$250.00.

Lot #403. Blue crystal bottle and stopper, 5" [12.7 cm], the bottle with eight feet, the stopper, with its dauber, intaglio cut with roses, bottom signed *Czechoslovakia* in a oval. Est. $200.00-$300.00.

Lot #404. Yellow crystal bottle and stopper, 4.6" [11.7 cm], the frosted base covered with a metal frieze and a green jewel, dauber lacking, bottom signed *Czechoslovakia*. Est. $400.00-$550.00.

Lot #405. Pink crystal bottle and stopper, 7.7" [19.6 cm], both bottle and stopper cut into an indentical fashion, base with six points, bottom signed *Czechoslovakia*. Est. $300.00-$400.00.

Lot #406. Blue crystal bottle and stopper, 4.8" [12.2 cm], the bottle encased in blue jewels, dauber lacking, bottom with *IRice* paper label and signed *Czechoslovakia*. Est. $400.00-$550.00.

Lot #407. Clear glass bottle and clear and frosted stopper, 6.9" [17.5 cm], the man caressing the woman's hand, with lovebirds at base, the top with roses and with a cut out portion at center, apparently unsigned. Est. $350.00-$450.00.

Lot #408. Large clear bottle with red crystal stopper, 4.9" [12.5 cm], the bottle cut into an octagonal star shape, the stopper of tiara form, dauber lacking, bottom signed *Czechoslovakia*. Est. $300.00-$400.00.

Lot #409. Clear crystal bottle and red crystal stopper, 4.4" [11.2 cm], the round bottle highly cut, the stopper cut with two flowers, with its dauber, bottom signed *Czechoslovakia*. Est. $350.00-$450.00.

Lot #410. Clear crystal bottle and stopper, 5" [12.7 cm], the stopper intaglio cut with the figure of woman in a plumed hat, dauber lacking, bottom signed *Czechoslovakia* and with partial *Morlee* label. Est. $400.00-$500.00.

Lot #411. Gigantic clear crystal bottle and partially frosted stopper, 9.8" [24.9 cm], the bottom highly cut, the stopper molded with a lady holding aloft a bouquet of flowers, cut out portions to the stopper, with its dauber, apparently unsigned. Est. $1,000.00-$1,500.00.

Lot #412. Frosted glass box and cover, 6.3" x 3.5" x 3" [16 x 8.9 x 7.6 cm], showing a swimmer on the two sides and a nude woman on the top of the box, bottom marked *Czechoslovakia* in the mold. This is very rare. Est. $1,000.00-$1,500.00.

Lot #414. Pair of clear glass bottles in a hat, 2.6" [6.6 cm] total height, one stopper with dauber and one without, signed *Czechoslovakia* with a paper label. Est. $350.00-$450.00.

Lot #415. Jeweled ring dish in green crystal, 1.6" tall [4.1 cm], the top shows a goddess surrounded by two cupids playing instruments, in a metal holder decorated with multicolored jewels, signed with the Hoffman butterfly. Est. $500.00-$750.00.

Lot #416. Smoke glass bottle and clear glass stopper, 2.7" [6.9 cm], the front of the bottle with an elaborate frieze of butterfly wings with opalescent and pink jewels, with its dauber, bottom apparently unsigned. Est. $600.00-$750.00.

Lot #413. Moser deep violet glass bottle and stopper with long dauber, 8" [20.3 cm], the bottle molded with a band of women warriors, the stopper with a stylized band, unsigned. Est. $800.00-$1,200.00.

Lot #417. Pink crystal bottle and clear crystal stopper, 7.7" [19.6 cm], the bottle cut in a basket motif, the stopper molded and cut in a flower basket motif, with its dauber, bottom signed *Made in Czechoslovakia Exclusively for Paris Decorators.* Est. $800.00-$1,200.00.

Lot #418. Yellow crystal bottle and stopper, 5.2" [13.2 cm], the stopper molded with flowers, the base impressed with the image of a lady in a fancy dress, probably unsigned. Est. $500.00-$600.00.

Lot #419. Yellow crystal bottle and stopper, 6.4" [16.3 cm], the stopper a three sided pyramid with intaglio cut flowers on one side, with its dauber, bottom signed *Czechoslovakia* in an oval. Est. $200.00-$300.00.

Lot #420. Amber glass perfume bottle and stopper, 6.4" [16.3 cm], the stopper intaglio cut with four flowers, the base highly cut, bottom signed *Czechoslovakia*. Est. $300.00-$500.00.

Lot #421. Amber crystal bottle and glass stopper covered in metal, 6.5" [16.5 cm], octagonal well for perfume, the stopper set with brilliant stones, with its dauber, unsigned. Est. $750.00-$1,000.00.

Lot #422. Moser perfume bottle and stopper in amber crystal, 6" [15.2 cm], with female warriors bearing bows and arrows, signed *Moser Carlsbad Made in Cecko-Slovakia*. Est. $400.00-$600.00.

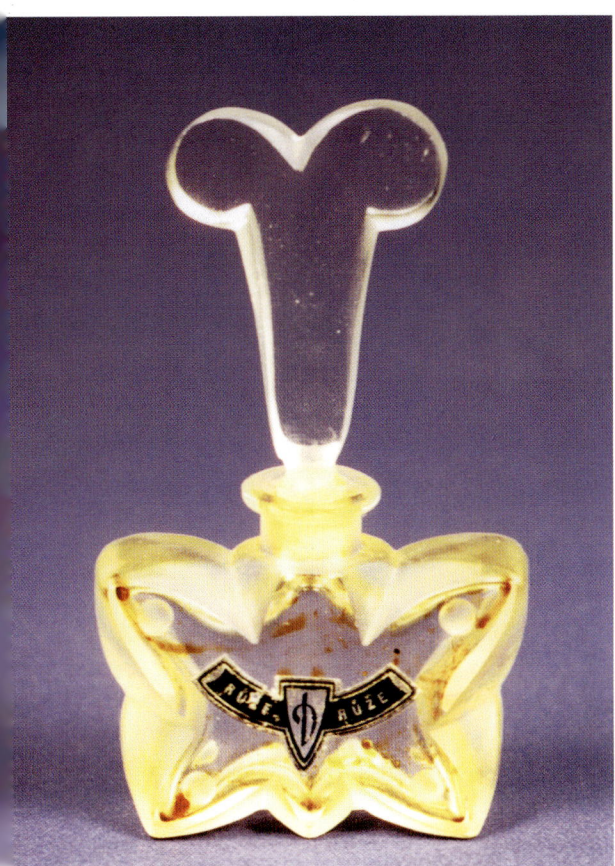

Lot #423. Beautiful clear and frosted bottle and stopper in the shape of a butterfly, 4.2" [10.6 cm], the stopper is in the shape of the butterfly's antenna, unsigned, label says *Ruze*. Est. $400.00-$500.00.

Lot #424. Green crystal bottle and stopper, 4.5" [11.4 cm], the base with ten sides and stopper with six, on a metal base with green and red stones, with its dauber, signed *Czechoslovakia* with a paper label. Est. $500.00-$600.00.

Lot #425. Very huge pink glass bottle with clear stopper, 12.5" [31.8 cm], the stopper intaglio cut with flowers and two butterflies, the bottle cut with nine feet, dauber lacking, signed *Czechoslovakia* in a oval. This is among the tallest Czechoslovakian bottles we have seen. Est. $1,000.00-$1,500.00.

Lot #426. Blue crystal bottle and magnificent clear stopper, 5.8" [14.7 cm], the base highly cut, the stopper intaglio molded with flowers and cut out in a tiara form, bottom signed *Czechoslovakia.* Est. $800.00-$1,200.00.

Lot #427. Beautiful blue crystal bottle and stopper, 8.7" [22 cm], the stopper with a design of a lady with garlands of flowers and with cut-out portions, with its dauber, signed *Czechoslovakia.* Est. $800.00-$1,200.00.

Lot #428. Opaque lapis lazuli crystal bottle and stopper, 5.6" [14.2 cm], in the shape of two open crysanthemum flowers, excellent variation in color to the glass, with its dauber, unsigned. Est. $800.00-$1,200.00.

Lot #429. Blue glass bottle and stopper, 5.2" [13.2 cm], the bottle molded with two maidens on front and back, dauber lacking, base with the Hoffman butterfly. Est. $800.00-$1,200.00.

Lot #430. Blue crystal bottle and clear crystal stopper, 7.4" [18.8 cm], the bottle with six feet all faceted, the stopper designed as a woman holding a bouquet of flowers, with cut-out portions and intaglio molded with flowers, with its dauber, bottom signed *Czechoslovakia* in a line. Est. $1,000.00-$1,250.00.

Lot #431. Ingrid beautiful set of three pieces of malachite glass, the perfume bottle 7.6" [19.3 cm], original atomizer, dauber lacking to perfume and with a short stopper, each piece is unmarked but bearing the *Ingrid* label. Est. $1,000.00-$1,500.00.

Lot #432. Ingrid malachite dresser box, 3.4" x 5.2" [8.6 x 13.2 cm], the cover featuring an Art Deco nude in a stylized pose, bottom bearing the Ingrid Czechslovakia label. Est. $1,000.00-$1,500.00.

Lot #433. Malachite glass bottle and stopper, 5.4" [13.7 cm], molded to resemble a cloud with the stopper of the same shape, bottom with Czechoslovakian label. Est. $2,000.00-$3,000.00.

Lot #434. Massive blue crystal bottle and stopper, 10.5" [26.7 cm], the massive stopper a prism, dauber lacking, reduction to lip of bottle, bottom signed *Czechoslovakia.* Est. $600.00-$750.00.

Lot #435. Enormous clear crystal bottle and stopper, 10.6" [27 cm], the stopper molded with bluebells, with its long dauber, bottom signed *Czechoslovakia* in a circle. Est. $1,000.00-$1,250.00.

Lot #436. Beautiful blue crystal bottle and stopper, 6.4" [16.3 cm], the bottle of triangular form cut with a sunflower, dauber lacking, bottom signed *Czechoslovakia.* Est. $500.00-$650.00.

Lot #437. Pink crystal bottle and stopper, 6.9" [17.5 cm], an unusual V-shaped design on an oval base, signed *Czechoslovakia* in an oval. Est. $600.00-$750.00.

Lot #438. Massive peach bottle and stopper, 8.5" [21.6 cm], the stopper with six feet, the stopper intaglio cut with a bird and a lady welcoming it, bottom signed *Czechoslovakia.* Est. $1,000.00-$1,500.00.

Lot #439. Clear crystal bottle and stopper, 7.4" [18.8 cm], the bottle of oblong shape on two feet and cut with step facets on the side and fan shaped facets on the front, the stopper intaglio cut on both sides with an elegant 18th century couple engaged in a formal dance, dauber absent, apparently unsigned. Est. $1,000.00-$1,250.00.

Lot #440. Large blue bottle and stopper in the shape of a duck, 6.3" [16 cm], the bottle an irregular form shaped like a duck's body, the stopper his head with red eyes on either side, bottom signed with paper label. Est. $2,000.00-$3,000.00.

Lot #441. Violet crystal bottle and stopper, 5" [12.7 cm], the base highly cut, the stopper cut with a star and of tiara form, bottom signed *Czechoslovakia* in an oval. Est. $350.00-$450.00.

Lot #342. Clear crystal bottle and stopper, 5" [12.7 cm], the stopper intaglio cut with a goddess and cupid carrying flowers, signed *Czechoslovakia* in an oval. Est. $200.00-$350.00.

Lot #443. Blue crystal bottle and clear crystal stopper, 8" [20.4 cm], the bottle standing on two feet, the stopper impressed with roses, dauber lacking, bottom signed *Czechoslovakia* in an oval. Est. $300.00-$400.00.

Lot #444. Smoke colored crystal bottle and clear crystal stopper, 6.9" [17.5 cm], the stopper molded with a large pointsettia blossom surrounded by smaller flowers, dauber lacking, bottom signed *Czechoslovakia*. Est. $400.00-$500.00.

Lot #445. Very large clear crystal bottle and stopper, 8.4" [21.3 cm], the bottle cut with three circles and with cut out portions, with its dauber, bottom signed *Czechoslovakia*. Est. $350.00-$450.00.

Lot #446. Tall pink crystal bottle with clear glass stopper, 8.4" [21.4 cm], the stopper of tiara shape with flowers, dauber lacking, bottom signed *Czechoslovakia*. Est. $500.00-$750.00.

Lot #447. Very tall clear bottle and stopper, 9" [22.9 cm], the bottle and stopper highly cut in an abstract motif, with its dauber, bottom signed *Czechoslovakia* in an oval. Est. $600.00-$750.00.

Lot #448. Clear crystal bottle and green crystal stopper, 5.6" [14.2 cm], the stopper intaglio cut with tihe figure of a male lute player, dauber lacking, signed *Czechoslovakia* in an oval. Est. $250.00-$350.00.

Lot #449. Clear crystal bottle and stopper, 6.8" [17.3 cm], the stopper molded with the beautiful face of a woman in an evening gown, with its dauber, bottom signed *Czechoslovakia*. Est. $500.00-$750.00.

Lot #450. Peach glass bottle and clear and frosted stopper, 6.2" [15.7 cm], the bottle cut with many facets, the stopper of tiara form intaglio cut with the figure of a man and woman courting, some pink and green stain, dauber lacking, probably unsigned. Est. $1,200.00-$1,500.00.

Lot #451. Clear crystal bottle and pink crystal stopper, 4.5" [11.4 cm], the stopper of tiara form and with its long dauber, bottom signed *Czechoslovakia* in a circle. Est. $400.00-$500.00.

Lot #452. Elegant and huge rose colored crystal bottle and stopper, 7.5" [19 cm], the bottle cut with eight sides, the stopper intaglio cut with a goddess and cupid, signed with the Hoffman butterfly, and with a paper sticker. Est. $1,000.00-$1,250.00.

Lot #453. Spectacular pink jeweled bottle and stopper, 5.3" [13.4 cm], in a metal jeweled base with pink opalescent stones, metal neck also with a stone, bottom signed *Czechoslovakia* in a line. Est. $1,500.00-$2,000.00.

Lot #454. Clear glass bottle in the shape of a dolphin with a green tail, 8" [20.3 cm], realistically molded, bottom signed with a paper label. This model is quite rare. Est. $1,500.00-$2,000.00.

Lot #455. Green glass bottle with clear glass stopper, 7.5 [19 cm], the bottle impressed with a large green glass medallion, the stopper a beautiful nude maiden walking amid flowers, dauber lacking, bottom and metal neck signed *Czechoslovakia*. Est. $1,500.00-$2,000.00.

Lot #456. Amber crystal bottle and stopper, 4.2" [10.7 cm], the stopper adorned with a nude, the bottle encased in metal and jeweled all around with red stones, dauber lacking, apparently unsigned. Est. $1,500.00-$2,000.00.

Lot #457. Dark green crystal bottle and stopper, 4.7" [12 cm], the bottle of atypical oval shape, the stopper also oval and intaglio cut with an image of a peacock and its long feathers, dauber lacking, signed with the Hoffman butterfly. Est. $800.00-$1,000.00.

Lot #458. Turquoise glass bottle and stopper, 4.7" [12 cm], etched and cut with an arrow design, with its dauber, bottom signed *Czechoslovakia* in an oval. This color is quite rare. Est. $400.00-$500.00.

Lot #459. Hoffman jeweled clear glass bottle and amber stopper, 6.8" [17.2 cm], the bottle decorated with five panels of amber and lavender jewels, the stopper shows a goddess blowing bubbles to Cupid; signed with the Hoffman butterfly. Est. $2,000.00-$2,500.00.

Lot #460. Hoffman's Leda and the Swan pink crystal bottle and clear crystal stopper, 4.4" [11.2 cm], the bottle with Leda and the Swan, the stopper with a classical scene, dauber lacking, both bottle and stopper signed with the Hoffman butterfly. Est. $1,000.00-$1,500.00.

Lot #461. Pink crystal bottle and stopper, 5" [12.7 cm], the stopper intaglio cut with a figure climbing up a hill, with its long dauber, signed with the Hoffman butterfly. Est. $600.00-$750.00.

Lot #462. Clear and frosted crystal bottle and stopper, 8.3" [21 cm], the bottle cut with a pretty design of flowers, the stopper with its dauber and showing two dancers, with cut out portions, apparently unsigned. Est. $600.00-$750.00.

Lot #463. Huge blue crystal bottle and clear crystal stopper, 9" [22.9 cm], the bottle of octagonal shape and highly cut, the stopper intaglio cut with a design of two birds and a nest, bottom signed *Czechoslovakia* in a line. Est. $500.00-$600.00.

Lot #464. Beautiful green malachite bottle and clear glass stopper, 6.4" [16.3 cm], the bottle molded with a nude on both sides, stopper molded as a bouquet of flowers, with its dauber, bottom signed *Czechoslovakia* with Nasco label. Est. $3,000.00-$4,000.00.

Lot #465. Green glass bottle and clear and frosted glass stopper, 7" [17.8 cm], the asymmetircal bottle beautifully decorated with green glass stones and pearls, the stopper with flowers and with its dauber, bottom signed with *Morlee* label and *Czechoslovakia*. Est. $2,000.00-$2,500.00.

Lot #466. Statuesque clear crystal bottle and stopper, 8.4" [21.4 cm], the stopper intaglio cut with an elegant lady admiring a bouquet of flowers, the stopper is further molded to conform to the shape of the portrait, dauber lacking, signed *Czechoslovakia.* Est. $750.00-$1,000.00.

Lot #467. Very rare black and red and white slag glass perfume bottle and stopper, 5" [12.7 cm], beautifully patterned symmetrically around the bottle, with its dauber, unsigned. Est. $1,000.00-$1,500.00.

Lot #468. Green crystal bottle and clear crystal stopper, 6.5" [16.5 cm], standing on four jade glass cut feet, set with four green glass roses, the stopper a large iris blossom, dauber lacking, apparently unsigned. Est. $1,000.00-$1,200.00.

Lot #469. Clear crystal bottle and stopper of brilliant turquoise crystal, 5.7" [14.5 cm], the bottle standing on turquoise feet with a border all around the bottom of turquoise medallions, glass beads around neck, unsigned. Est. $3,000.00-$4,000.00.